G000255122

West from Salisbury

33109 seen at Skew Bridge, Salisbury working the return empties to Meldon Quarry on 12 May 1987. Although not as glamorous as passenger workings the stone train turns to Whatley Quarry or Meldon were where most of us Salisbury crews 'cut our teeth'. The turns were all manned by a driver, secondman and guard. For the guard there was the preparing of the train, calculating the load and the coupling and un-coupling of the loco when running round at Westbury or attaching the loco at Whatley. For the secondman it was assisting the driver whilst running round, looking out for signals, helping the guard (especially if he was a senior man, then you would do the coupling/un-coupling), making the tea (junior guards would be expected to do this also) and the best bit, having a go at driving. The driver looked after the train, secondman and guard, and took overall responsibility, but was not expected to make the tea. (*Andy Read*)

West from Salisbury

150 Years of the Railway to Tisbury and Gillingham

Steve Chislett & Mike Pearce

Millstream Books

Dedicated to the memory of
Derek Malcolm Pearce
(27 January 1961-21 July 2004)
a Salisbury railwayman for 22 years –

and to all Salisbury railway workers past and present

Salisbury guard Derek Pearce standing next to his favorite class 50, No.50016 *Barham.* (*Willy Wiltshire*)

All royalties from the sale of this book will be donated to the Stars Appeal at Salisbury District Hospital which funds extra care and equipment over and above that provided by the NHS.

First published in 2009 by
Millstream Books, 18 The Tyning, Bath BA2 6AL

Set in Times New Roman and printed in Great Britain by Short Run Press Limited, Exeter, Devon

© Steve Chislett and Mike Pearce 2009

ISBN 978 0 948975 87 5

British Library Cataloguing-in-Publication Data:
a catalogue record for this book is available from the British Library

All rights reserved. No part of this publication may be reproduced, stored in a retrieval system, or transmitted in any form or by any means electronic, mechanical, photocopying, recording or otherwise, without the prior permission of Millstream Books.

Foreword

What an honour to be asked to write a foreword to this marvellous record of the local railway – although it did make me realise that I must have first moved to Salisbury around the time of the 100th anniversary! Which, of course, set me thinking about my own memories.

I can just about remember standing on the footbridge at Milford Hollow, (I now realise that was by the 95m 20ch milepost) and being surrounded by steam. Certainly I recall running to the bottom of the school playing field to see what we were told was the last steam train. I also remember some friends trying to turn half pennies into pennies out by Petersfinger. One of them gashed his leg falling down the bank and had to miss a football match – it seemed a real disappointment at the time but now one realises how lucky they were.

Later was the first big trip to London and seeing those people writing something down at Basingstoke and Woking, and my father explaining the rudiments of collecting train numbers. We went to a test match at Lords but the scale of Waterloo and the idea that you went on another small train actually under the Thames were nearly as exciting.

And then a couple of hard days' work in the yard at Salisbury one winter in the employment of Messrs Clarke, Lush & Co. Sadly student jobs today don't provide the character-forming nature of shovelling frozen coal before dawn.

Then the start of a long gap although the early part was broken by the occasional weekend attempt to get back home via Reading and Basingstoke. Surely there was just as much weekend engineering work with replacement buses then? Overton ... Whitchurch ... Andover ... Grateley ... Salisbury still has a welcome rhythm to it.

Much later I came back, though now in a very different role. No longer a passenger or observer I had a more important role as the Director at Waterloo. Soon I was off on visits to local boxes – Eastleigh, Salisbury, and then down the line to Yeovil Pen Mill where I met signaller Alan Cox who had joined the railway around the time I was born. Such history and continuity, and how lucky to be involved at what I am sure is just the beginning of a period that will be as exciting as much of what is described in this book.

I also went to the maintenance depot at Salisbury, then in the hands of Balfour Beatty, and a plan was formed to start to bring it back 'in house'. That led to one of the more sobering experiences of my career. Was it in the *Railway Club* at Salisbury or in the *White Hart*? Anyway I came bouncing down from London to announce the plans only to be told in no uncertain terms by the maintenance staff that it was me that was coming back to them. Railtrack had been something of an absentee landlord and it was only the experience and loyalty of the local staff that had kept the railway going – and we had even called them contractors! Oh dear.

But let's move on to that exciting future. Network Rail has a massive funding programme for the next five years. We are putting back some of the double track on the route to Exeter. We have plans for longer trains and longer platforms to meet demand. The route via Micheldever is being upgraded to a higher gauge for the important freight traffic from Southampton, and the diversionary route via Romsey is also being improved. A new cab radio system is coming. The layout at Salisbury is being upgraded. Better passenger information systems are coming.

Overall the railway is in a much better place than it has been for decades. I am sure we will leave our grandchildren the best possible legacy for them to be able to celebrate the 200th anniversary.

Robin Gisby
Director, Operations and Customer Services,
Network Rail

Introduction

This book is a celebration of 150 years of the provision of railway services between Salisbury and Gillingham, and a tribute to those who have spent much of their lives ensuring that they give the best that they can, not solely for the passengers but also for their colleagues. Although the present-day operation is vastly different from that applicable when the railways were first set up, railway staff have always been expected to adapt to technical advances.

The original decision to 'single' the line on much of the track between Wilton and Pinhoe was a drastic change resulting from implementation of the 'Beeching Report' in the 1960s that affected a number of lines and services in Britain with many complete closures. Along with the singling of the line between Wilton and Gillingham, the stations at Wilton South, Dinton and Semley were closed on 7 March 1966, leaving Tisbury as the only intermediate station on the Salisbury to Gillingham section. All freight facilities and trains have also been lost from not only the MoD sites at Dinton and Chilmark, but from Gillingham (fertiliser trains) and, the latest casualty, the closure of the English China Clay facility at Quidhampton in May 2009.

But despite all this the 'West of England' line has kept going and indeed prospered from an increase in passenger numbers over the years. A new passing loop was installed at Tisbury and by the end of 2009 a new running loop of over three miles will be in operation at Axminster. The unique nature of the line with long single sections has caused many problems, associated mainly with late running, but has helped create a 'family feel' to the route as we all work hard together to keep the service running.

Gone are the days when you were able to gain employment on the railway purely because your relatives already worked there. Today, the initial selection of new employees is based on assessments by computers where accuracy is combined with reaction times. Although this is a very different approach, there are still families working on the railway such as Steve Anderson along with his sons Brian and Tony who are drivers at Salisbury. Other families that work on the 'West of England' line include brothers Andy and John Beavis, both drivers at Salisbury, and we must not forget Derek Pearce, now deceased, his brother Nigel, a guard at Salisbury, and Mike, a Salisbury driver, who has devoted much time and effort to the content and success of this book. John Say, a signaller for Network Rail at Salisbury Area Signalling Centre, has been a railwayman for almost 39 years, continuing the family association with the railways in a different area of operations to his father, Tom. Gemma Hirst originally started on the railway straight from school in the S&T department with Balfour Beatty and has now joined her father Colin as a commercial guard at Salisbury with South West Trains.

This book is not the result of my personal work but of the efforts and special enthusiasm of a number of railway employees and notably Mike Pearce. He spent many hours interviewing characters who worked on the railway and all credit is due to him for the results. Sincerest thanks go to driver Paul Abbott who willingly assisted Mike in the difficult job of selecting the published photographs from thousands provided. All photos in this book have come from members of staff past and present or from local enthusiasts, who have given their permission for them to be published, for which we thank them. Thanks must also go to Andy Beavis and Kris Jendesen for their help and encouragement, Ian Smith for his excellent historical knowledge, Gary Pollard and Donna Ridgewell for their research, and John Say for note-taking, mainly in the form of sponsorship! My task was simply to edit and arrange the chapters. It has been a great pleasure for me to be given the honour to help produce this book as a tribute to railway colleagues past and present. With the wealth of experience and knowledge held by those individuals employed by South West Trains and Network Rail passengers can rightly feel confident that their journeys are in safe hands and being dealt with by true professionals.

Steve Chislett
Editor

Editorial Note

The passages of text that link the various memories in the book have been written by Mike Pearce and are shown in italic type.

The Origins of Salisbury (Fisherton) Station

Saturday 2 May 2009 marks 150 years since the first passengers set foot onto the new platform at Salisbury (Fisherton). It is, however, quite remarkable that it had been constructed at all partially because it had been the last of three railway stations and lines built by two railway companies.

The Romans were probably the first people to recognise the importance of the area with two main routes crossing at Sarum. The most important one being the road from London to the west, this road had gone unnoticed by railway promoters at this time. These were normally local MPs and business men wanting to make money out of the new railways. This was the case with Salisbury except that the MPs and others were in Southampton and they in turn had a little help from Napoleon?

During the Napoleonic wars and after Napoleon's defeat in 1815 many schemes were put forward for a ship canal from London to the south coast in order to move military traffic without fear of attack from the French in the English Channel. These schemes failed mainly because of water supply problems over the South Downs. The people of Southampton took advantage of this constant threat of war at a public meeting held on 26 February 1831 in the town hall which led to the formation of the Southampton, London & Branch Railway & Dock Company. Southampton, with a population of 19,000, was once described as a port of poor reputation and the only other town of any size between London and the south coast along the projected route was Winchester, having a smaller population of only 8,000. It had been realised early on that they would have to look elsewhere for more revenue. The 'Branch' in the title was to be a line from Basingstoke to Bath and Bristol, the 'Dock' meaning the construction of a larger deep-sea port. The former never managed to gain an Act of Parliament.

On 31 August 1835 an Act was successfully passed for the Great Western Railway (GWR) to build a line from London (Paddington) to Bath and Bristol. The Southampton Company became very disillusioned and dropped 'Branch Railway & Dock Company' from their title to become the London & Southampton Railway (L&S). One of the many objections to the proposed line had come from the people of Bath refusing to be served by a company with Southampton in its name. Company names and titles were important issues at the time. The L&S decided to console itself by dropping all thoughts of the Bristol area and turned its attention to 'new unlooked for' income in the form of other lines on the south coast. The Act for the railway from London (Nine Elms) to Southampton terminus was passed on 31 January 1835 with the first trains running the full length of the line on Monday 11 May 1840.

The first branch to be built with the 'new unlooked for' income in mind was from Bishopstoke (Eastleigh) to Gosport. By rights this should have been their first priority as it was, after all, the base for the Admiralty on the south coast and the initial reason for a railway in the first place! The first train ran on 29 November 1841. At around this time the L&S changed its name to the London & South Western Railway (L&SWR) following a short period of being called the South Western Railway.

The L&SWR now started to look towards Salisbury but more as a local line, with no intention of going beyond the city. The wounds of the earlier defeat over Bath and Bristol still ran deep. The branch left the main line, as with Gosport, at Bishopstoke but this time facing north from the upside (west side) and headed to Salisbury by way of Chandlers Ford and Romsey, then running into a terminus at Milford next to the Southampton road. It had been very clear that the L&SWR never had any intention of constructing the line any further west, short of building it through the middle of Salisbury cathedral!

This was the first railway to arrive in Salisbury when the line opened to goods traffic on 27 January 1847 with the first train consisting of wagons laden with coal to be distributed to the poor. The junction layout at Bishopstoke was such that Salisbury was never intended to receive traffic to and from London! The normal method of working was for goods and passengers to change trains at Bishopstoke; however, the first passenger train to depart from the Milford station on 1 March 1847 was bound for London and carried only a few passengers and dignitaries.

At a public dinner in the *White Hart Hotel* that evening one of the speeches hinted that all of Salisbury's railway needs had been met as it was pointed out that the railway would be able to despatch men and munitions for the army and also the two very valuable commodities of coal and salt could be carried to the city at a much lower cost. During the building of this line the railways of Great Britain had gone through the period of time known as 'railway mania' when no less than 576 Acts were passed authorising almost 9,000 miles of railway.

One of these Acts passed in 1845 was the Wilts, Somerset & Weymouth Railway (WS&WR) with the line leaving the GWR near Chippenham and with a branch to Salisbury. The L&SWR didn't appear too concerned at this time, mainly because of the financial depression that was starting to take hold but also because they seem to have become involved in far too many other schemes. The one that concerns us most was the indecision over the most suitable route to Exeter. On 26 March 1846 a meeting was held at Sherborne town hall to promote the London, Salisbury and Yeovil Railway. Also in 1846 the L&SWR gained an Act to build a further line from Basingstoke to Salisbury (Milford) and a short branch from Laverstock to connect up with the WS&WR at its Fisherton terminus. On 22 July 1848 the Salisbury & Yeovil Railway (S&YR) was authorised to run from the L&SWR Fisherton station that had been authorised in 1846. On 1 June 1848 the Southampton & Dorchester Railway was opened and operated by the L&SWR; this line had been promoted by a Wimborne solicitor, Charles Castleman. Due to the way the route wound its way through the countryside the line gained the name 'Castleman's corkscrew'.

It was this line that split the L&SWR in two. Castleman insisted that the best route to Exeter and the West Country was a coastal one via Dorchester but it didn't include Weymouth. This was evident at Dorchester where the original station was built facing the west and Exeter, not Weymouth. Castleman probably thought that with the L&SWR routes set firmly in Southampton that his would be the chosen way; however, the majority of L&SWR directors and landowners preferred the inland route known as the 'central line' and this group was led by the eminent engineer Joseph Locke. Not only did Locke build the main line from Nine Elms to Southampton but he also lived in Honiton. Although the central line was the shortest route between Exeter and London, Castleman somehow managed to win two separate ballots. This may have been because with the line now opened to Dorchester the construction mileage to Exeter would have been around 50 miles as opposed to the 120 from Basingstoke. The directors seem to have totally ignored the fact that the central route was by far the shortest and also followed the main turnpike road of the day as previously mentioned.

By 1854 the people of Somerset and Dorset had become rather fed up with waiting on the L&SWR and looked at building the line themselves. In 1855 they had a helping hand from Parliament. The L&SWR gained a Consolidation Act on 14 August 1855 but for the second time in the L&SWR's history Parliament had inserted a clause that required the company to honour an earlier 1853 pledge to extend to Exeter within five years. The penalty for not completing this pledge was to stop payment of all dividends. At long last this was the moment when all warring sides came together, with the company holding a special meeting on 16 January 1856 that reached agreement on the central line route. The L&SWR's financial state was still very poor and because of this the company came to an agreement with the S&YR that this company would construct the line and the L&SWR would operate it, in return for 45% of the gross receipts. The L&SWR also cut the construction cost of the Basingstoke to Salisbury line by building it as a single line with the second road to be laid when more money was available. As the original 1846 Act for the line had lapsed – they usually lasted only two or three years – the WS&WR had jumped in and built their terminus on the site that the L&SWR had intended for their own station. The WS&WR having been built to a broad gauge, the company did, in fact, offer to lay a third rail inside its own line to provide a dual gauge so that the S&YR, working with the standard gauge, could use the WS&WR station. This was not uncommon for the day, but the GWR had taken over WS&WR operations and the old rivalries had been reignited.

The original 1846 Act would have authorised the L&SWR to enter the station at Fisherton on the level but Salisbury Corporation objected on the grounds that it would interfere with the prosperity of the city. In 1857 a South Western bill resulted in changes to the land and the alignment of the railway which sited the L&SWR's Salisbury (Fisherton) station where it stands today, built on the south side of the GWR terminus with a bridge over Fisherton Street as opposed to a level crossing and no physical connection with the GWR at this time. A transfer shed had been constructed for the transhipment of goods traffic between standard and broad gauge wagons, a very common practice of the day. A new public road was constructed from Fisherton Street to the station and called South Western Road.

The new station opened on 2 May 1859 and the people of Salisbury now had three ways of getting their goods to and from their city, yet the L&SWR directors still appeared blind to the importance of the route. All

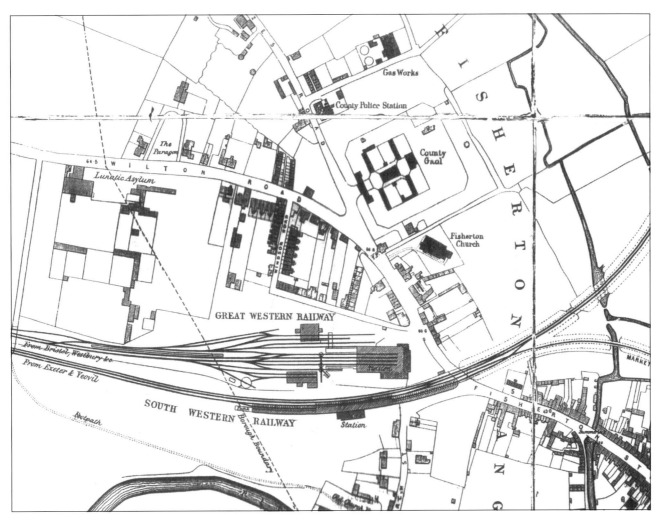

The 1860 Ordnance Survey map of Salisbury station. (© *Crown Copyright, 1860*)

London-bound trains departed from Salisbury heading north-east, crossing first over Fisherton Street Bridge then passing through Fisherton Tunnel and Tunnel Junction where six of the ten London-bound trains in the 1859 timetable were routed via the double track curve at Laverstock to Milford, still the L&SWR main station at this time, and passengers then had to change trains at Bishopstoke! The other four services in the timetable took the single-line, northern route via Andover, again changing trains but on this line at Basingstoke. Incredibly, the shorter, single-line route via Basingstoke took the same time as the longer Bishopstoke route. The entire route to Exeter (Queen Street), now called Exeter Central, opened to traffic in 1860 and yet in spite of competing with its old rival, the GWR, the L&SWR went on to take over and build new lines in the deep south-west which added to the prosperity of not only the L&SWR but also the city of Salisbury. The importance of the route that was nearly

overlooked by the L&SWR can be seen when looking at the company crest (*below*) which depicts five shields: on the top left London, below it Southampton, on the top right Salisbury, in the middle right Winchester, and at the bottom right Portsmouth.

One hundred years later the Beeching Report of 1963 indirectly sealed the fate of the L&SWR route to the west. The report found that the now Southern Region route to Exeter was, in fact, far more profitable than the Western Region route so when the report recommended the transfer of the line west of Wilton to the Western Region the Southern did not object.

(*left*) Jim Beavis, who was a wheeltapper, is pictured standing by the building on the west end of platform 2/3 which was first used for storing and heating the seat-warming pans. It was then used until its closure as the station fitters' stores (downstairs) and mess room (upstairs). Jim was the grandfather of Andy and Jon Beavis who are both current Salisbury drivers. (*Jon Beavis collection*)

(*right*) Thomas H. Coles, great grandfather of Robin Coles, who started on the L&SWR at Salisbury in 1875 as a guard. (*Robin Coles collection*)

They thought it would survive the Beeching axe, which meant that they could then concentrate on modernising their other main lines. Once again their old rivals, the GWR got their claws out and eventually set about closing branches, goods yards, stations and withdrawing services, but more bizarre than that was the singling of the double-track line that cost a lot more to achieve than the annual maintenance costs. To this day this has continued to hinder the growth and prosperity of the route.

The modern-day trunk roads, A36 and A303, have reached saturation point. Things have come full circle. 150 years after the opening of Salisbury (Fisherton) station the importance of the station is only now being realised as it forms a very important and busy interchange between London Waterloo, Exeter and at times Paignton or Plymouth, with Cardiff, Newport, Bristol, Bath, Southampton and Portsmouth. To complete the story, when the L&SWR outgrew the facilities at Nine Elms they moved closer to the centre of London, just across the river from the Houses of Parliament, to their new terminus. In recognition of their origins they named it Waterloo!

Ian Smith
driver for South West Trains at Salisbury

(*above*) Driver Ian Smith makes running repairs to a window that will not remain shut on Salisbury's resident bubble car 960012 (ex W55028) using no more than blue paper and a hammer; it actually worked! The unit is at Waterloo after working a route-learning special from Salisbury via Chertsey and Hounslow on 5 April 2006. (*Mike Pearce*)

(*above*) The front of the original 1859 building at Salisbury as seen on 20 February 2009. The lower floor now houses the ticket and administration offices (on the left), the signalling relay room (with darkened windows), and the entrance to the driver and guard standards managers' offices (far right) which occupy the upper floor. (*Mike Pearce*)

(*below*) A platform view of the original 1859 buildings taken in 1983. (*Colin Hall*)

(*left*) Tisbury station photographed in March 2009. The journey from Salisbury to Tisbury takes 12 minutes by train compared to 35 minutes by car with no hold-ups. Poor road access is one reason for the station remaining open. (*Mike Pearce*)

(*below*) Tisbury station in the early 1970s looking in the up direction, with all the track lifted from the down side and platform loop; just the single up line remains (as it does today). This photo was taken before P.J. Parmiter & Sons, agricultural machinery merchants founded in Tisbury in 1890, took over the area in the foreground. Their yard came right up to the outer face of the deserted island platform, with their buildings coming to roughly the nearside platform edge. This is probably the only area of the whole route from Salisbury to Exeter that could not, at present, be put back to double track. You cannot get a view of the station like this anymore as apart from all the lorries parked awaiting repair in what is now a heavy goods vehicle garage, trees and bushes have grown up to obscure the view. (*Paul Edwards*)

(*left*) A platform view of Gillingham station photographed in 1984. (*Colin Hall*)

(*below*) A fine postcard view of a bustling Gillingham station, c.1900. A number of smartly-dressed passengers are awaiting trains on both platforms and a porter has just pulled a trolley-load of parcels across the board walk. Note the Dando wind pump seen above the funnel of the locomotive. This pump was sited on the up side and drew water from a deep well for the station's use, mainly for the locomotives from the hose in the near right foreground. The buildings have changed little over the years compared to the photo above except for the disappearance of one chimney stack and a few chimney pots. Two luggage trolleys stand unused in each photo, though of different design. (*by kind permission of Gillingham Museum*)

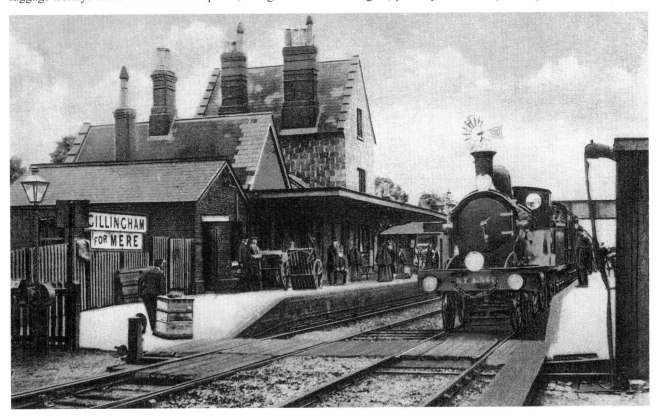

(*right*) Semley station was opened on 2 May 1859 by the Salisbury & Yeovil Railway and closed on 7 March 1966 under the Western Region of BR. It was built to serve Shaftesbury but earned its keep by becoming, in 1871, the first wholesale depot in Wiltshire for supplying milk to London. (*Colin Hall*)

(*below*) Dinton station seen in 1984 under private ownership, though the small cabin on the far end of the platform was still being used by the MoD railway staff. The station had an unremarkable life being opened by the Salisbury & Yeovil Railway, like Semley, on 2 May 1859 and closed by the Western Region of BR on 7 March 1966. During the Second World War the American air force opened a large depot and warehouse complex nearby, which was taken over by the Admiralty and the RAF after the war and generated traffic for the railway right up until 1995. (*Colin Hall*)

Salisbury Motive Power Depot over the Years

The first steam shed was sited near the west end of the present platform 4; a second three-road shed was built close by in 1885 on land that is now the car park. Both sheds were lost in the station rebuilding of 1901, becoming the seven-road West Yard. At the same time the LSWR built a large, and for its time, modern ten-road shed further west, its pedestrian access coming from Cherry Orchard Lane, and nearly opposite the GWR shed which was situated in Ashfield Road. The GWR shed closed in 1950 with its men and work transferring over to the Southern shed; the WR engines were serviced at the SR shed but were re-allocated to Western sheds, mostly Bristol. The old GWR shed buildings became the Southern Region's stationery distribution warehouse for about 10 years. The building in parts has become part of the trading estate that now covers the whole area. At its height, the steam shed at Salisbury boasted some 250 pairs of men (drivers and firemen), with approximately 40 cleaners and 300 shed staff, whilst the guards came under the jurisdiction of the Stationmaster. One could only start on the footplate over the age of 21 and definitely by the nature of the work, no women! The 'job' was very manual, dirty and hard work. Most of the staff were local, the furthest coming from Dinton!

Salisbury had shrunk from 200 pairs of men in 1965 to only 60 drivers and 30 secondmen (12 of whom were relief drivers) in 1975. This was achieved without any compulsory redundancies through men transferring to other depots or departments, natural wastage and not filling jobs when drivers retired; anyone over 60 was offered early retirement and many of the older drivers took up this offer. The steam shed closed in February 1969, the remaining drivers, firemen, running foremen, time keeper, list clerk and depot manager moving to Salisbury station. The depot was downgraded to a signing-on point. The shed staff did not fare so well and many were made redundant, only a few making the move to the station (as fitters, shunters or platform staff). Some did manage to get jobs with the Permanent Way Department, others with the Signal & Telegraph department. With the coming of the 159 units Salisbury has been revitalised and become a train crew depot once again with 118 drivers, 88 guards, a depot manager, 4 driver standards managers,

4 guard standards managers, support clerk, 4 operational re-source managers (loco foremen), cleaners and another 101 staff employed in the new train care depot.

Although there had been no restrictions on women applying for footplate jobs with British Rail it wasn't until 1979 that the door was opened by Annie Winter who applied and became the first BR woman driver in 1983; by transferring to Salisbury in 1991 she also became Salisbury's first female driver. Donna Ridgewell became Salisbury's second, transferring in 1998, with Val Coote being the first local Salisbury woman to become a driver at the depot shortly after. Salisbury now has eight female drivers including our first mother and daughter drivers, Sue Colson and Beth Nash, as well as 13 female guards. One can now become a driver from all walks of life; Salisbury train crew depot is made up of people from all across Britain, from other depots within South West Trains, and also with origins from around the world: West Indies, Italy, Africa, Ireland and the European Continent. A big culture change for Salisbury as only 20 years ago, if you came from outside the county of Wiltshire you were a foreigner!

Gary Pollard
driver for South West Trains at Salisbury

Salisbury guard Sue Edwards seen as she covers the train crew foreman job on 3 October 2005. Sue started on the railways at Shrewsbury in 1990 and found that the people with most prejudice against women were the wives of the men who worked there! In 1993 she worked the royal train to Aberystwyth taking Prince Charles, though she did not get to meet him as it was 03:00 in the morning and the prince was asleep; but he could rest assured that all the staff were wearing their hats! Sue transferred to Salisbury in 1999. (*Gary Pollard*)

(*above*) 34024 *Tamar Valley* comes on shed for the last time on 8 July 1967. 34089 *602 Squadron* has just dropped her last fire and is going on shed where the fitters will remove her rods and motion and she will await her fate. (*Derek Barrett*)

Posing on a USA tank engine are, from left to right, Salisbury cleaners Bob Hardy (who later became a driver at Salisbury, now retired), Frankie Paulk (who transferred to the Permanent Way Department when the shed shut), Dave Barnet (likewise, now deceased), Pete Adlam (likewise), and Freddie Hunt Jnr. (who became a driver at Eastleigh, now retired). Looking out of the loco cab is Glyn Wells who moved away to work on the Ravenglass railway. (*Steve Anderson*)

(*above*) Alfie Watts and Willy Wiltshire storm away with 35028 *Clan Line* in October 1986, past the site of the old steam shed. (*Paul Abbott*)

(*left*) Salisbury driver Alfie Watts (right) and fireman for the day, driver Willy Wiltshire, before working one of the many steam specials to Yeovil Junction and back. Alfie has since retired but Willy is one of our most senior drivers still. (*Andy Beavis*)

(*left, above*) A view of the rear of Salisbury steam shed taken on 26 March 1969. The staff had all moved out and this was the day the contractors started to demolish the site. During the process they managed to knock a huge chunk of the side retaining wall into Churchfields Road (*see the photo below left*), luckily without harming anyone but blocking the road for a day. The whole roof of the shed caught alight – a health and safety nightmare now with the asbestos! Roger Long (driver standards manager at Salisbury) remembers seeing the shed ablaze as a kid: 'I lived in Nursery Road on the other side of the running lines opposite the sheds; the fire engines came dashing down our road, sirens blaring, only to find they all had to reverse back out as we lived in a dead end that was of course on the wrong side of the tracks! I remember laughing as they reversed out; it just seemed funny seeing fire engines going backwards with their sirens sounding. I went to the bottom of the road, with many other residents, and watched the fire and the eventual arrival of the fire brigade who did a swift job of extinguishing the blaze.' (*E.W.Fry from the Colin Hall collection*)

(*left, below*) While being demolished the contractors found the supporting wall to the steam shed to be fragile resulting in its collapse into Churchfields Road. The poor state of the wall has been a factor in why the area has not been developed over the years. (*photo by kind permission of David Mant*)

(*above*) Cherry Orchard Lane on 4 March 2009. The site of the steam shed is just waste land.
(*below*) Taken on the same day, Churchfields Road where the wall collapsed in 1969; the dip where this occurred can still be seen. (*both photos Mike Pearce*)

Mike Pearce

Driver at Salisbury

My interest in railways started when I was a young boy. Our house was near the main line from Salisbury to Waterloo. On hearing the magnificent Merchant Navy or West Countrys powering their way up the bank away from Fisherton Tunnel my brother, friends and I had just enough time to run to the bottom of our road and watch the mighty beasts pass us at Bishopdown on their way to London.

My ambition to become a train driver came about on a trip out by train to Swanage when I was about five years old. Remember how summers used to be, when a trip to the beach was followed by a night of sheer agony trying to not lie on your sunburned back in bed? Well, after this trip I could not sleep, not from pain, as the day was the one wet day I can remember as a child, but from sheer excitement. The Salisbury to Wimborne line was still open and we were walking along platform 4 at Salisbury towards platform 6 where the train to Bournemouth West was waiting to depart. At the end of platform 4 the platform dips to ground level before rising up again to the bay platform 6; it was whilst in the dip that a train to Waterloo was leaving from platform 2. I stopped in awe and watched as the streamlined West Country started to move. I grabbed my Dad's hand tight with a mixture of fright and excitement as the engine struggled for grip and the huge wheels started to spin violently. There was a huge whoosh of steam from this massive living machine as she grappled with her heavy load and the wet rail. Slowly she took control and moved away in a show of pure power, fantastic! I was now definitely hooked and as far as I was concerned there was no need to go to school anymore; I was to start on the railway as a driver the next day!

All that night I could not sleep, it was worse than waiting for Christmas day I was so excited. Finally morning came and I rushed downstairs, had my breakfast and kept on at my parents about taking me to 'work'. I must say my Dad did a great bit of parenting that day and shattered my dream gently and without tears as he skilfully explained to me that in 11 years' time I could be a train driver if I worked hard at school!

Those years passed by and I tried my hardest at school, but there were a few setbacks along the way. The first setback came in July 1967 when steam came to an end and the shed at Salisbury closed. My uncle

Ron 'Tigger' Pearce, who was a driver at Salisbury, told me that it all looked pretty gloomy with many people losing their jobs. 'I can see no future in the railways now', he said.

I was also disappointed that there were no more Bulleids, but their replacements were just as exciting to us youngsters. The Class 42/3 Warship diesels sounded just wonderful, but along came setback number two – they, too, were withdrawn!

I was now getting interested in other forms of transport and my future on the railways had to contend with maybe lorry or bus driving! Then came the strongest contender yet and the only one truly that could have stopped me joining the railways ... football! I loved it, and now I was to become left-winger for Salisbury City and England.

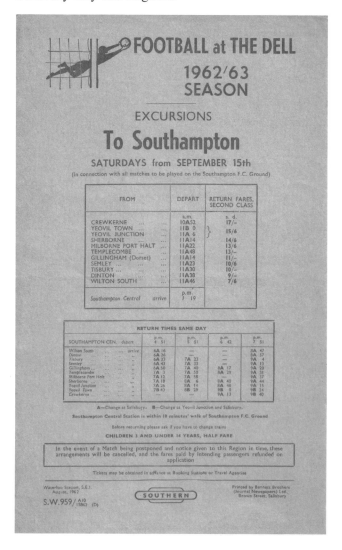

So it was on 15 July 1974, subject to passing a medical, that I signed on for work at British Rail as a traction trainee, not a left-winger (apparently I was not as good as I thought at football!). I had kept the family name going on the railways, as my grandfather and uncle had both been drivers at Salisbury. My two younger brothers, Derek and Nigel, also entered into the spirit of things and joined the railways when they were old enough, both becoming guards at Salisbury. Nigel is still working alongside me now but unfortunately Derek, a well-liked and respected member of staff, passed away at the age of 44 after 23 years' service.

I remember walking into the mess room on my first day and quietly taking a seat. Immediately I was asked: 'Why on earth have you come to work on the railways? This place is going to shut'. Seven years on from the closure of the shed confidence still seemed low. But one of the younger men, Brian Lucas, said: 'I started in 1961 and all I've ever heard is that this place is going to close; don't worry mate, you'll be here as long as some of these old moaners, as long as you can stick the shift work'.

So here I am, 35 years later, one of those lucky people who does a job they enjoy. I have worked with a great bunch of people, past and present, and across the network.

It only seemed fitting that with the 150th anniversary of the opening of Salisbury station at Fisherton we took the opportunity to record some of those 'railway stories' that we all have and also to share some of our own photos, and to help raise funds for the Stars Appeal at Salisbury District Hospital charity to boot.

Salisbury driver Tom Pearce worked from 1901 to 1950 and was joined by his son Ron in 1939. Tom was working the paper train to Yeovil one day in 1946 with a nearly new Merchant Navy loco; as they went through Buckhorn Weston tunnel, just after Gillingham, the driving rod bucked, bringing the train to an abrupt halt but somehow without derailment. Another day Tom was leaving the shed at Salisbury with a King Arthur to work to Waterloo when embarrassingly he collided with a T9 coming on shed, driven by his son Ron! This photo was taken in 1955 by Tom's son Roy Pearce, my Dad! (*Mike Pearce*)

Here I am waiting to leave Salisbury on 18 June 1990 for Exeter with 50007 *Sir Edward Elgar.* I always found 50007 to be all show and no go. The last 50 I worked on was 50033 *Glorious* with the 15:15 Waterloo to Exeter, as far as Salisbury on 7 March 1992: the last 47 was 47703 working the 15:34 special from Salisbury to Waterloo on 17 June 1993; and the very last loco-hauled train 33116 on a Sandite working with 016 Hap unit from Salisbury to Basingstoke and return on 18 October 1993. (*Keith Usher*)

Bob Bailey

Railwayman at Salisbury

The first recollections come from Bob Bailey who was the timekeeper and cabin cleaner when I started. He always kept our mess room spotless and crews from other depots were quite jealous! Bob was a very kind and jolly man, a keen gardener, modeller and owner of a tortoise, which we, as kids, would try and feed with leaves as we passed by Bob's back garden!

Bob started his railway career in August 1946 and went on to serve on the operations side for 50½ years. His first duties were as callboy/messenger. This involved taking call tickets to off-duty drivers/firemen at their homes advising them of a change in their duty or informing them of their next duty if they had been on a rest day. Sometimes Bob would be required to knock the driver up for early starts, a delicate job of tapping on their house window loud enough to wake the driver but not the rest of the family! He would also, if required, call in the breakdown crews (there were at the time two drivers for the steam breakdown crane that was kept on shed) and take or pick up messages, mail and parcels from Salisbury station.

Bob progressed on to engine cleaner and well remembers the hard dirty work that entailed and using the highly suspect 'Weaver' steam cleaners. Bob can re-member when the GWR steam shed across the road shut in 1950 and the men transferred over; there was a lot of resentment as many SR men were put back years because of the high seniority dates that the GWR men had.

Bob slowly carried on up the promotion ladder to become a fireman but then suffered a bad accident that left him unable to go out on the main line due to failing eyesight (unlike today, glasses were not allowed to be worn; if they had, then Bob could have carried on to become a driver). This setback did not put Bob off the railways and he worked with the shed drivers. These were very often drivers who were taken off the main line for different reasons, some at that time because of shattered nerves caused by driving trains to Waterloo during blackouts in the war and being bombed on their journeys. Together they would move the loco, after it had been coaled and watered, onto the table, position it up or down and put it in the shed if repairs were needed or in the yard ready for its next turn of duty. Bob said during the '50s there was plenty of work for the shedmen especially on late turn because of the number of freight trains that ran through the night and required engines.

Trains leaving Salisbury each night, Monday to Friday

10.30pm	Freight to Yeovil
11.02pm	Freight to Basingstoke
11.10pm	Eastleigh mail
11.15pm	Aberdare coal empties
11.45pm	Fast freight to Exeter (from Nine Elms, crew/engine change, 60mph)
12.30am	Freight to Yeovil
01.10am	Empties to Severn Tunnel Junction
01.30am	Freight to Yeovil
01.35am	Freight to Eastleigh
02.10am	Stone empties to Exeter
02.30am	Stone train to Woking
02.55am	Newspapers to Wimborne
03.05am	Newspapers to Exeter
03.25am	Newspapers to Yeovil
03.30am	Empties to Avonmouth
04.20am	Freight to Bournemouth
04.30am	Freight to Yeovil
04.35am	Freight to Basingstoke
05.00am	Vans to Yeovil
05.00am	Stone train to Havant
06.30am	Freight to Yeovil

Bob used to help out with many different jobs around the shed. These included helping to dispose of engines when they came on shed for the top link firemen (this involved cleaning the fire and smokebox out, raking out the ash pans and watering the engine). He used to help his friend Tom Crowley wash out the boilers, a job that was preformed on each loco every 10 days (this was done using chemicals that were flushed through the boilers). The boilers would be checked by the boilersmiths by crawling through the boiler looking for leaks. The steamraiser would then be required to re-light the loco's fire; it would take over six hours to get the engine back in steam, plenty of time for Bob to clean the loco.

Bob recalls the many other different staff employed at the shed. Along with the 123 drivers, 130 firemen, and cleaners, there were shed fitters who carried out heavy repairs on the engines on day shifts, running fitters who worked shifts and did light running repairs as and when required, coal stage staff who used to shovel coal from wagons onto the conveyor belts that then dropped the coal via the chutes into the engines' tenders. This could be a gruelling job in winter as water was sprayed onto the coal to keep the dust down and this in turn made the ground messy and slippery. With the coal stage up higher the prevailing wind used to whip down through it, and even though each night two 21-ton coal wagons were emptied, the poor men still felt the cold!

There were labourers that did all odd jobs, storemen, office staff, running foreman, time clerk, shed foreman, shed master, sand furnace staff. Bob remembers the last sand furnaceman only by his nickname of 'Amigo' – he was Italian and only got the name because he called everyone 'Amigo'. He was a builder by trade, but in the great freeze of 1963 there was no work for him so he took the vacant sand furnace job!

One of the worst jobs at the shed was carried out by Zaker Waters and his mate Claude Davies. They would be in charge of keeping the drains and filter beds clean and clear of ash; this involved a lot of disappearing down deep dirty holes. They also had to shovel all the ash and clinker from the engines that was dumped on the ground or in the pits by the firemen, into wagons. The wagons were then taken on the short trip to the market branch and the ash and clinker was sold to a local builders' merchant who would then make building blocks out of it.

Bob remembers going down the Market House branch with wagons full of seeds for Dunn's seeds, coal for the coal merchant and the small generating station, timber, ash, clinker for the builders' merchant, hops and grain for the brewery; it was for a time a very busy little area.

By 1965 Bob was one of the last shed firemen. All cleaning of engines was done on overtime by firemen as no cleaners were now being employed by BR and there was a marked run down of engines and shed. Many of the Waterloo to Exeter trains were now worked with Warship class diesels along with Nine Elms and Exmouth Junction crews. The WR Hymeks started to appear on the Bristol to Portsmouth Harbour services and this along with the Bournemouth branch closure meant many steam engines were on shed all day and withdrawal of engines that needed attention began in earnest.

Bob recalls the following years 1966-1969 with great sadness. With the closure of the steam shed looming anyone over the age of 60 was offered early retirement which many accepted. Other staff left to join the Permanent Way or the Signal & Telegraph Departments, but at least on the motive power side there were no forced redundancies as BR agreed to 'carry men over'.

Bob well remembers Saturday 8 July 1967 and recalls watching the last engine off shed, a 73 standard with a Nine Elms crew, working the 6.30pm to Waterloo. Next day saw the arrival of many engines. Each engine was sold at £2,000 unless it had a copper firebox which

would command £3,000! Each would be stripped and stored at Salisbury; the fitters removed the rods and motion so as not to have to oil them for their last journey. Bob saw himself given the job of removing the coal from the tenders and bunkers of the engines using a mobile crane. The coal was sold off locally.

During 1968 the contractors came in and started dismantling the whole depot. The last of the steam engines was towed away in March and all the remaining shed staff were made redundant unless lucky to be re-graded, or taking up posts at Salisbury station. In February 1969 the motive power signing-on point moved to Salisbury railway station and the depot was no more.

Bob was fortunate to secure a post as timekeeper/depot cleaner at the new Salisbury signing-on point, which was (and still is) housed on the upper floor of the main station buildings. Until his retirement in February 1997 Bob kept the drivers mess room at Salisbury in pristine condition, renowned for his efforts across the region, and it was generally recognised that Salisbury mess room was the cleanest on the South Western.

One of Bob Bailey's last jobs was in charge of *HMS Redundant*, a small mobile crane that was used to remove coal from the withdrawn engines, most of it being sold on to local merchants. Bob is seen on what also became known as 'Bob's Baby' along with Mr Blackman, the final Shed Governor (on the left), and Charlie Goodridge, the running foreman that day, 18 November 1967. (*Bob Bailey collection*)

(*above*) Bob Bailey cleaning 34100 *Appledore* in November 1965, a health and safety nightmare! On the right, note the fire devil behind him; these were looked after by the shed labourers, but many a young cleaner honed their fire-building skills on these crude heaters. (*Bob Bailey collection*)

(*below*) 70004 *William Shakespeare* was a surprise visitor on shed in early 1967. Bob Bailey took this photo as he was shed fireman that day and relieved the Fratton crew to service the loco and turn it, ready for them to work back. (*Bob Bailey*)

(*above*) 34089 *602 Squadron* coming off the turntable on the last weekend of steam, 8 July 1967. It will be Bob Bailey's job to remove the coal from 34089 bunker after she has breathed her last. (*Derek Barrett*)

(*below*) 75138, seen withdrawn at Salisbury shed in November 1967. The push bike belongs to shed driver Fred Stoodly and was put by the engine so as he could effect a quick getaway, as this day he was off to watch Salisbury City play football when he clocked off at 14:30. Unfortunately, when he came to leave, some wag had hidden the bike high in the roof rafters. Fred could not retrieve the bike so ran to the football ground, missing the first 15 minutes. When he returned after watching Salisbury lose, his bike was positioned back beside 75138! Bob Bailey swears it was not him who moved the bike. (*Bob Bailey*)

George Lynam

Railwayman at Salisbury

Next we hear from retired driver George Lynam, a true character who could write his own book on his career; maybe he will soon, but for now we have the following snippets.

I started on the railways on 5 April 1956 and although I was on the bottom rung I felt proud to wear the uniform, so proud in fact that it hurt – I was riding home on my pushbike the first week and was trying so hard to keep my hat on that I rode straight into a parked car in Devizes Road, no mean feat as there weren't many around then! I soon learnt to stuff paper in it to help keep it on my head.

I started as a callboy taking messages to and from the station and steam shed, taking duty call-ups to drivers and firemen at their homes, and also waking drivers on early turns. It wasn't long till I got promoted to cleaner. This was dirty work but it was great to see the loco you had just cleaned go off shed all shiny. I spent two years as a cleaner before I was promoted again to 'passed cleaner'; this meant I could now prepare and dispose engines as well as clean them. The bonus of being a passed cleaner was that you would do trip workings off shed to East Yard, the Market branch and Milford Goods, not far I know but exciting after being in the shed for two years. I can remember being quite excited waiting for the call from pointsman Harry Barker to come up to the exit signal with our M7 tank on my first trip working to East Yard and Milford Goods. Harry Barker would sit in a small wooden hut near the shed exit and inform the signalman what the next engine coming off shed was for and then with the signalman's permission he would call over the tannoy system 'Engine on 7 road come up to exit signal'. Now Harry sometimes forgot to turn the tannoy off, with everyone on shed and householders in the vicinity being treated to a badly sung song, out of tune whistling, or his mumbling and moaning!

You were very often paired up with drivers who were 'put back'. These were drivers who were taken off main line duty because of stress, or medical problems. After the war there were a few drivers who could not face driving because they had pushed themselves and kept going, although they hated driving, especially to Waterloo with the constant fear of bombings, the railway being a prime target. The one thing these drivers did have was years of experience and I learnt a lot from them, not only about driving and firing but also about life. You would also be put with some of the passed firemen, these were firemen who were passed to drive, so they were upgraded to driver and I was upgraded to fireman. Men like Ted Noakes, Den Bentall, and Ren Judd, all were fun to be with as they were young and they would help and show you how to fire well.

One of the other jobs the cleaners and firemen had to do was every now and then go with Bill Giddings, the shed cleaner's foreman, over to the GWR shed which had closed in 1950 but had for at least seven years lain dormant; it was like stepping back in time, very quiet and eerie. We would go over to clean *Box Hill*, tank No.5603 and Queen Victoria's coaches that were stored there. There were many items just left lying around that would be worth a fortune today! I cannot recall what happened to it all when the shed became the Southern Region's distribution centre for all its stationery needs; someone got lucky I expect! The WR turntable was also used whenever our turntable was being serviced.

I got promotion to fireman on vacancy list 47 (*see the photo opposite*) in 1959. I went into the bottom link which involved working freight trains mostly to Basingstoke, Yeovil and Westbury, again not far, but it could easily take 12 hours to get there and back –your driver was your paymaster!

My next promotion saw me move up into the mixed traffic link; in this link you worked, say, a passenger train to Waterloo, took your engine light to Nine Elms for servicing then worked a freight back to Salisbury. These were usually fast fitted freights, that had almost passenger timings or sometimes the return milk empties from Vauxhall to Chard or further afield. Of course you could work a freight or milk up either to Nine Elms, Feltham or Vauxhall and then a passenger or parcels back down – there was a fair bit of variation in the link.

The best thing about the link though was that you got to work the ACE. For me this was the most thrilling experience of all that I have had on the railways. The Atlantic Coast Express was of course the Southern's premier train (to anyone west of Basingstoke, naturally) with a heavy load of up to 15 coaches and a demanding schedule – it sorted the men from the boys! I was lucky

BRITISH RAILWAYS
THE RAILWAY EXECUTIVE
SOUTHERN REGION
MOTIVE POWER DEPT.

SALISBURY.——————DEPARTMENT

——————STATION

IN YOUR REPLY PLEASE
QUOTE THIS REFERENCE

Fol.59.

2491 A

27th.March 1956.

      Referring to your recent request for employment here as an
Engine Cleaner, please report here at 7.20am. Wednesday 4th. prox.,
for purpose of travelling to Eastleigh for Eyesight and Medical
Examinations.   You should travel by 7.47am. train, changing at
Romsey – a free ticket to cover your journey will be handed you at
this office.

      After examinations the doctor will give you a letter which
should be brought to me without delay and if the result of such
examinations are satisfactory arrangements will then be made for
you to commence work at a date suitable to yourself.

                                          F. W. Dale

Mr. G.P.Lynam,
9 St.Martins Close,   Shedmaster.
Barford St. Martin.

ACKNOWLEDGMENT

Application for vacancy as FIREMAN   advertised in
                              (grade)

Vacancy List No. 47   received.

To MOTIVE POWER
    SUPT. WATERLOO   5 JAN

                                        Office Stamp.

To be completed by applicant.

One thing we had that the Western didn't was the humble white cloth. On arrival at Cardiff we would hand over our engine to the Western men along with a bundle of white cloths. We would have our break, usually a cup of tea and cakes from the fantastic bakery down the road, whilst the Cardiff crew serviced our engine. They would hand it back in pristine condition with a perfect fire and a bunker full of the best coal, such was the power of the white cloth.

From 1960 to 1968 the railways took on a very sad look, everything was run on a shoestring, with maintenance cut back to the bare minimum, and we were all unsure of our futures because of Beeching. Diesels were replacing steam and we had the Warships on many of the Exeter to Waterloo trains. For a fireman there was not much to do on them except for keeping the steam heat boiler running and making the tea!

as one of my regular drivers was Percy 'Golden Boy' Marsh, a true engineman of the highest quality. Percy could work the up 2.09pm ACE from Salisbury to Waterloo in 75 minutes, a feat that quite a few drivers could do, but the difference with Percy was that if you were his fireman you would work hard only as far as Andover after that you would just put a bit on now and then and by Woking you were a spectator. Driver Ted Trickett was another excellent engineman. You knew that working with either of these two men and putting in a good performance you would be rewarded with some spectacular running and a fantastic feeling of true team work between you, the driver and the engine – pure magic.

I finally moved into the Spare Gang which involved working everything everywhere! It meant I also got to work on the GWR engines over to Severn Tunnel Junction and Cardiff. The footplate on all the GWR engines were basically the same. I worked on Castles, Halls, Manors, 2800s and 72 tanks – they were all well looked after and rode like sewing machines, smooth and quiet. Unfortunately we never got on the Kings as they were banned from working on the Southern narrow gauge, although one or two did slip through the net and caused a bit of damage along the way. I seem to recall one getting through to Fratton where it remained for over a week while the powers that be decided how to get it back to the WR with the minimum of damage.

Percy Marsh, on the left, was one of Salisbury's finest enginemen. George Lynam was his regular fireman and they are seen here on 34087 *145 Squadron* on the coal stage at Salisbury shed in April 1967. (*George Lynam collection*)

Salisbury shed, as we all know, stayed till the end. I can remember my last firing job on the main line, Waterloo to Salisbury semi-fast along with Percy Marsh on 34013 minus its *Okehampton* nameplates, and I'm not ashamed to say I was so upset that all the great times I had so far on the railways looked like they were coming to an end, that I cried.

Salisbury shed from July 1967 was a depressing place with all the engines stored there awaiting their end, along with all the men who had worked on them not knowing their future. I, like many others, made the big decision to move away and get a driving job as it would be years before any driving positions would become vacant at Salisbury, if you were lucky to be kept on, as it turned out BR did not make anyone compulsorily redundant on the footplate side, the shed staff and fitters not faring so well. I moved to Woking and started driving electric units, some of which were older than the steam engines that I had been on before! I had a great time working with the other drivers there; the railway spirit prevails wherever you are.

I moved back to Salisbury in 1991 to find it in the same run-down state – the Class 50s were on their last legs and the 47s that had come to replace them were not much better – but it was good to see many familiar faces from the steam days, now, like me, senior drivers (sounds better than old). At least for a while I was back driving real trains.

Then in 1994 we switched to our own dedicated fleet of 159s, nowhere near as exciting as a Merchant Navy, but clean, smooth-riding, quiet and reliable, and so it was that these were the final traction along with the 170s that I worked on till I retired in 2006, although there was the totally unexpected chance to work on steam again and I was lucky to work on 777 *Sir Lamiel*, 828 and 34027 *Taw Valley* during their visits in 1997 along with driver Den Bentall. We had a great time; mind you it knackered me and was somehow a lot harder.

The final years were some of the most traumatic of my railway career and 1998 tested my resolve to the limit when I endured two serious operating incidents, that, thanks to my experience of the routes and practices, saved two potentially life-threatening accidents. On top of those I had three people commit suicide by jumping in front of my trains, one a fellow member of staff from Salisbury. A year to try and forget. I had good support from my family and fellow staff which helped, and along with the strong character building I had gained over the years, I was able to carry on.

I can honestly say I thoroughly enjoyed my time on the railway and would do it all again. I have had the privilege to have worked and made friends with some excellent enginemen over the years, many of whom I still see, as I organise quite a few reunions and what is nice is that present-day staff come along and meet all us oldies and share stories – we all have loads!

When George Lynam was on his last firing job on 3 July 1967 he could not contain his disappointment and shed a tear. 34013 *Okehampton* was the engine, seen here at Basingstoke, and Percy Marsh the driver. (*George Lynam*)

A picture taken in 1949 at Salisbury shed with driver Ern Butt standing on the running plate of a Drummond class T14 No.462. These locos were built by the L&SWR at Eastleigh for the Waterloo, Bournemouth and Salisbury expresses and for their time were powerful engines. They were nicknamed by crews 'Double-breasters' because of their four cylinders set alongside each other, but were more commonly known as 'Paddle-boxes' as when originally built they had a lower running plate and one single long splasher, which was removed from 462 in 1930. Oliver Bulleid wanted to withdraw the class in the late 1930s. However the outbreak of war gave them a stay of execution and they proved invaluable for moving the heavy military traffic, petroleum tankers and evacuee specials. 462 received her wartime black livery with sunshine yellow lettering in 1941 and remained so adorned until her withdrawal in February 1951. A bomb at Nine Elms destroyed No.458 in 1940, 445/59/60 were cut up at Dinton, and the rest of the class were cut up at Eastleigh. Note also in the photo the tannoy speaker above the engine, which delivered the magically singing and whistling tones of pointsman Harry Barker to depot staff and nearby residents! (*Mick Price collection*)

George Lynam on his last day at work, 9 April 2006, with driver Roger Macey on the left and guard Ted Parrish on the right. They were honoured that day to see a railway miracle, one of George's legendary tea bags finally got wet and a brew was made. The date of this momentous occasion is still scribbled on our mess room wall! (*George Lynam collection*)

(*below*) The Atlantic Coast Express with 35028 *Clan Line* in charge at Weybridge where the train would be at full speed, around the 90mph mark. For George Lynam his favourite job was working the ACE and the pinnacle of his railway career; nothing could beat the sheer exhilaration of team work between driver, fireman and engine. This photo was taken by Mick Foster, a driver from Guildford, specially for George who was the fireman on the footplate, the driver being Percy Marsh.

George Lynam also organises excellent reunions which attract large turnouts. Here is a selection of photos from these events.

(*above*) A group photo taken at the 2006 reunion. All were or are drivers unless otherwise mentioned:
Back row, from left to right: Willy Wiltshire, Pete Smerdon, Roger Luckins (then Operations Training Manager), Fred Johnson (traction trainer), Ken Day, Ren Judd, Bob Lawrence (guard), Chris Pelling, Keith Usher (Operations Manager)
Middle row, from left to right: John Dawkins, Pete Rebbeck, Ted Thornton, Eric Cave, Dusty Miller, George Lynam, John Cornelius (signalman Chard Junction), Dave Power, Barry Hayter, Bill Bailey, John Carter (head shunter)
Front row, from left to right: John Hartford (head of driver training) Mick Oakley (traction trainer) Jon Harding, Mike Pearce, Adrian Stewart, Bob Thompson. (*Geoff Birch*)

(*left*) John Carter (retired) receives a smacker from driver Ted Thornton (retired) at the 2008 reunion organised by George Lynam. John was head shunter at Salisbury and one of our biggest comedians; you had to have your wits about you when John was on duty, if you could find him! (*George Lynam*)

(*below*) Two long-suffering railway wives, Peggy Thornton and Shirley Wareham having a chat about anything other than railways at the same reunion in August 2008. (*Mike Pearce*)

Noel 'Tom' Say and John Say

Guard and Signalman at Salisbury

The next two accounts come from father and son, Noel and John Say. Noel, was a guard, and the ever youthful John is still a signalman at Salisbury.

Noel Say has been known as Tom since his army days. He was born on 1 December 1919 in Alderbury and began the family tradition of working on the railway. Tom's family moved from Alderbury to York Road, Salisbury at an early age.

I left school when I was 14 years old and started work as a baker's boy at Sutton's Bakery in Crane Street, Salisbury later moving to work as a milk boy at Cook's Dairy, based at Lower Bemerton on the western outskirts of Salisbury. I joined the army when I was 17 years old in 1936 and remained in the forces until I was demobbed in 1946. At that time I applied for a number of jobs including the Post Office and Southern Railway. As the Southern Railway responded first it was their offer that I accepted.

Starting as a carriage cleaner I was later appointed to the position of porter until I transferred to carriage shunter, eventually achieving promotion to the enviable grade of guard. I was able to complete 38 enjoyable years of satisfying but hard work and retired in 1984.

* * *

John Francis Say was born on 24 April 1955 and joined British Railways at, as he puts it, the 'tender' age of 15 years on Monday 21 July 1970, having left school the previous Friday.

I was appointed as a Salisbury messenger boy/junior railman which involved taking notices to the signalboxes or despatching them by train for Salisbury Tunnel Junction and Wilton South boxes. I remember on occasions cycling out to Wilton South and to driver's and guard's houses within reasonable distance of Salisbury station with urgent messages, especially regarding duty changes. Telephones at private addresses were nowhere as common as now and this was a cost effective way of delivering urgent messages. We would then return to the station with replies, particularly where overtime had been offered or a change of duty requested.

After about a year, Mr Owen Faisey, the Station Manager, decided to move me to platform duties but being 17 years old I was restricted to working early and late turns only. Duties included dispatching trains, cleaning toilets, subway, platforms, waiting rooms and dealing with the parcels handled by NCL. Early shifts started at 06.00 and we were responsible for unloading 'brutes' or trailers that would easily stretch from the parcel office that was sited in what is now the signalling relay room to the top of platform 5, virtually the whole length of platform 4. These parcels had to be placed in the correct spaces in the Parcels Office and checked with the delivery record for loading and delivery by the NCL van drivers. Special attention was paid to cleaning all brass knobs and handles, even in the toilets, and if there was a shortage of carriage cleaners we were expected to carry out these duties. We also covered Warminster station when required for platform and parcel duties. This particularly applied in the lead up to Christmas when there was a vast increase in mail and parcels especially from the military establishments.

After Christmas in 1972 I saw an 'exhausted' vacancy, one that was unfilled despite previous publicity, for signallers. I was accepted for training even though I was not yet 18 years old, as I would reach this age soon after completing the training. In 1973 I attended a three-week course at Beckenham Signaller Training School and my first appointment as a signaller was at Wylye signalbox between Salisbury and Warminster, qualifying for this one week after my 18th birthday when I 'passed out' for this location.

In 1975 I transferred to Wilton South signalbox until I moved in 1980 to Salisbury West box. This box, along with seven others, was closed in August 1981 when control passed to the new Salisbury Area Signalling Centre that had been built in a disused men's toilet block. Before the closure of the manual boxes in 1981 there was a personal and team pride in keeping all brass well polished along with the lino on the floors and every signaller did their bit to maintain the high standards expected if they were working on the cleaning day every Saturday. Signallers pulled all levers with a hand cloth to keep them clean. With safety in mind people wishing to visit a signalbox had to knock and wait to be invited in with the single word 'Enter'. The signallers at Salisbury West signalbox at closure were Ernie Foreman, Pete Steele and myself, with Derek Hopkins, Barry Lake and Albert Smith from Salisbury East box and Bob Blandford who acted as relief signaller for Salisbury. [Editor's note: John is

(*above*) Signalmen John Say, on the left, and Ernie Foreman work the then new Salisbury panel in 1982. (*Robin Coles*)

(*below*) WR pannier tank 4616 passing Salisbury West box in 1963 en route from the shed to Fisherton Yard to start shunting. Note the ¾ milepost on the side of the box; this is for milepost 83¾, the mileage from Waterloo, and is part of the Salisbury 'short mile' as milepost 84 is only about 100 yards west of here. (*Pete Warren*)

the longest serving signaller at Salisbury with a current total of 39 years due on 21 July 2009, quite an unusual achievement these days.]

One signaller, Pete Steele, decided that he didn't wish to transfer to the new panel and chose to train as a guard, a career that he stayed with until he retired in 2008. He was replaced by Bob Blandford who was a keen supporter of the scout movement and was twice elected as the Mayor of Wilton. He was also keenly involved in the 'Riding for the Disabled' scheme at Wilton and upon his untimely death a few years ago left large amounts of his legacy to Wilton Scouts who have built a new scout hut that can be seen from the train at Wilton South; funding for the 'Riding for the Disabled' centre at Wilton; and also for Wilton church. Bob received the MBE in recognition of all his hard work to improve facilities for Wilton residents. With a true interest in anything involving his home town he was, without any doubt, a very well respected person. He was also a personal friend who, as far as I am concerned, had a character that deserved that respect.

The Area Signalling Inspector at the time I was due to 'pass out' at Wylye signalbox was a Mr Kendall and I was scheduled to be authorised for signalling duties one week after my 18th birthday. Cliff Dunn, who had taught me the functions of that box, said: 'Don't worry, you won't need to get here until 09.00', and who was already there when I arrived? You've guessed, the Area Signalling Inspector – not a very good start, I thought to myself. Normally, most Inspectors would remain for a couple of hours to ensure that you dealt with everything safely but my Inspector stayed until the end of my shift. Despite my apprehension he passed me out and I was officially a qualified signaller just one week after my birthday.

On one occasion when I was working in Salisbury West box between 1980 and 1981 there was a freight train in the West Carriage Sidings and when the guard said: 'We're ready to go to Westbury', I pulled off the relevant signals and set the route. The locomotive shot off, leaving the rest of the train and guard's van behind much to the surprise and embarrassment of the guard whose expression had to be seen to be believed! It was the guard's responsibility to ensure that the train was complete and ready to go. Quickly I arranged to stop the train at the starting signal and received a call from the driver on the signalpost telephone asking why he had been stopped and I suggested that he look at his train, which was not a train but only his locomotive. His response is not printable but you can well guess the number of expletives during his call! The locomotive returned to collect the rest of its stock and it was ensured that all wagons and guard's van were securely tied on. I can still vividly remember the guard's face and recall that his expression was 'a picture'.

A scary moment for me was when John Morgan, who was a Salisbury signaller, was booked on at Codford as Automatic Half Barriers Attendant when I was at Wylye operating as the barrier attendant. Unknown to me, he had arrived early and parked his car well out of view and entered the permanent way hut that had replaced Wylye signalbox after it was demolished. He had positioned himself in the far corner of the hut, placed a wrinkly old man's mask over his face, and switched all the lights off. When I opened the door I shone my Bardic lamp to find the light switch and caught a glimpse of something in the corner. He said in a creepy voice 'What are you doing here, then?' Well, the fright still haunts me even now and I must have almost hit the ceiling it was so scary. John just could not stop giggling; he had thoroughly enjoyed himself, unlike me!

One of my scariest professional moments was when an employee was driving an electric tractor used for towing the 'brutes' across the barrow crossing, now lifted, at the London end of platform 4. These tractors had a habit of cutting out at the most inappropriate times and the driver had the misfortune to cut out while across the track. There was no chance of setting the signal back to danger and no way to contact the driver of the approaching express. Looking through the window of the signalbox I could see that the tractor driver was making no attempt to abandon the vehicle and taking no notice of the express. Despite the emergency application of the brakes on the train there was a terrific crash with the battery of the tractor flung into the air. The train came to a shuddering stop and I feared the worse, as I could not see the tractor driver. After a moment he appeared above the platform edge and I was so relieved; he must have got away with his life by seconds or inches.

John and I played football together for the Railway Social Club FC and I well remember our long chats about the morning's game when we were late turn on Sundays. Whereas I have lost my youthful looks and fitness, John has not and he regularly takes part in all sorts of physical activities to raise funds for various local charities and is rarely to be found without a sponsorship form on him, a legacy of his friendship with Bob Blandford I guess, but something for which John, too, deserves respect.

Salisbury East signalbox on 6 March 1981. Salisbury (opened in 1902) used an air pneumatics system with draw-slide-powered lever frames working signals and points through air pressure at 15psi pumped from the compressor in East yard to holding tanks outside East and West box. The system was also used at Grateley. (*Robin Coles*)

Salisbury East box photographed on 8 August 1983 just before it was demolished. (*Robin Coles*)

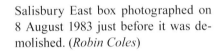

The end of Salisbury West signalbox on 27 September 1983. (*Robin Coles*)

(*above*) 50016 *Bar
ham* at Gillingham. The photograph was taken by driver Steve Anderson who was waiting in the siding to work the Gillingham to Ince and Elton fertiliser empties. His guard, Pete Steele, can be seen on the left, above the buffer stops,

(*right*) 73114 arrives at Salisbury working the 07:17 Waterloo to Salisbury special Christmas mail train on 8 December 1987. (*Keith Usher*)

John Hill

Guard at Salisbury

Next we hear from John Hill, or as we all knew him 'Lardy'. He was a good guard to have because not only was he good at his job but also a very funny man!

I started on the railways on 24 December 1954 at Milford Goods Yard in Salisbury as a junior number taker that involved taking the numbers of the wagons as they arrived, putting on the wagon labels and doing the yard stock returns. For this I was paid £2 9s 2d for a 44-hour week, 7.00am to 4.00pm Monday to Friday and 7.00am to 11.00pm on Saturday. On my first day there I had to see Arthur Cane the yard foreman; he had previously worked at Swindon and moved to Salisbury after the war. He asked me my name. I said 'John Hill, sir'. 'Ah, I knew a Lardy Hill at Swindon, so I will call you Lardy'. The name stuck and everyone called me Lardy right up to the day I retired!

Working in Milford with me were Morry Bethall, Johnny Williams and Dennis Judd, all of whom, like me, went on to become guards. We were always busy, as everything for the town came in by train and we got to know many of the local firms as they came and picked up their goods.

In 1957 I was promoted to goods porter in Fisherton Yard. Here, on the platform of the old GWR station, Boots the chemist used to take delivery and store agricultural medicine for use on farm animals. There was also Chapman Shipping Company, who dealt in animal hides, which were extremely heavy! Annett's China took crockery that came packed in straw within huge wire cages. In the goods shed Silcock's took in animal feeds, cattle cake, pig meal and chicken feed; this was then given out to the farmers who used to call in and pick it up, a very smelly area! From time to time we would receive a container from Wandsworth that was always difficult to get off the wagon, as it was so heavy. I used to really struggle winding the crane to get this one off. The container was for Radnor House, that was only up the road at the junction of Wilton and Devizes roads, and contained MoD stationery – goodness knows how many letters they must have been sending out! We used to get wagons come in from Scunthorpe's steel works; these were flatbed and had three containers on filled with basic slag which was picked up by farmers to spread over their fields. There was an art to getting these off the wagon and to discharging the slag into the

farmers' lorries; you would hook the containers onto the hand-worked crane, lift them off, swing the crane round and position the container over the waiting lorry. Now came the dodgy bit, you had to undo the bottom of the container with your shunting pole by pulling out four pins so the two doors could drop open and the slag would fall into the lorry – messy when you got it right with all the dust, but if the doors got half cocked you had to get in closer and struggle with the pins, usually with you ending up covered in the slag!

In 1959 I was promoted again to East Yard checker. This involved delivery of goods to the steam shed, the Signal & Telegraph and Permanent Way Departments, and working down the Market branch. I would make up a train that we would 'trip' to the steam shed and West Yard, this would be stores equipment ordered by shed storeman Fred Butcher and Permanent Way equipment for their stores in West Yard. The train was usually hauled by one of our M7 tanks with put back driver Les Millard and fireman Bob Bailey. Delivery into the shed stores was always a chore as I had to get Fred Butcher to sign for the goods and he was very precise and would check everything thoroughly. Mind you, he had a tough job keeping an eye on everything in the shed stores! Wagons for the S&T were put down the back road of East Yard as their stores were in Meadow Road; we unloaded the goods and let them slide down the embankment to their building! When working down the Market branch the load could be no more than five wagons because of the severe gradient and again with an M7 tank. This line was the shortest standard gauge railway in the country and remained in the hands of an independent company, the Salisbury Railway & Market House Co. Ltd, right until the line closed in 1964 and, indeed, it was still paying out dividends as high as 12.5% in the 1950s. It was wound up in 1965. We used to take coal mostly down to Associated British Malt for their burners to dry their malt, and to The Salisbury Electric Light Company for their generating station. Their coal came from Writhlington colliery near Radstock and was very small coal, almost like dust, which they burnt on revolving grates where once burnt it would fall through the grate and come out the other end. Ash from the steam shed was sometimes taken to The Building Materials Company who would make building blocks from it. Deliveries were sometimes made to W. Main & Sons, and Dunn's seeds.

All wagons were pushed down the branch from platform 6. There was a brake van just before the first set of points and this guarded the branch; it was kept locked. I would couple up to it then unlock it, go in and take off the hand brake and then we would push it into the siding out of the way, come back over the points and then go down the branch. Coming out was tricky as we had to go back down as far as the Electric Light Company siding blocks so as to get a run at the bank otherwise you would never get up! We would then go back light engine to replace the brake van as branch sentinel!

(*above*) An M7 tank going from Salisbury East Yard to the West Yard, viewed from the end of platform 6. This particular M7 had been allocated to Exmouth Junction shed for most her life and transferred to Bournemouth Central in 1963, which probably dates this photo to that year, during her transitional period. (*Mick Price collection*)

In November 1962 I became a goods guard in Salisbury 3 set with a pay rise to £8 9s 3d. I now had a bag that I carried around as did all guards. Nowadays it would be a Health and Safety nightmare as all it had in it was wood, paper, paraffin – all for making a good fire in the van! – tea can, cup, flags, detonators and a rubber washer for a vacuum brake pipe. Riding in the brake was very relaxing and at night when reading a book by Tilley lamp I am sure it was the fumes that made you drift off into a dream world.

In 1979 I was promoted to station chargeman at Andover; I really enjoyed my time there but it was short-lived as six months later, that September, I moved back to Salisbury as station supervisor. Again this was a job I enjoyed, especially working with Steve 'Ginge' Blackmore and Gareth Langford, both wonderful characters!

In 1985 I was made redundant and took the job of guards inspector at Salisbury. I did not like this job as I was in charge of men I had worked with for many years (and most knew more than I did) and at times would have to discipline some. I changed jobs, taking a pay cut, and became a Revenue Protection Inspector which got me out on the trains again, but I soon changed from that into the ticket office at Salisbury where I wound down ready for my retirement in 2000. I thoroughly enjoyed my time on the railways and met some wonderful people; you were never alone on there and everyone would help each other with whatever you wanted, someone always knew someone who could do it!

(*below*) John 'Lardy' Hill seen on a brake van that is a long way from home, in Salisbury East Yard in 1959. (*John Hill collection*)

Bernie Shergold looks back to get the tip to go from the guard whilst working a Salisbury to Yeovil special on 4472 *Flying Scotsman* on 16 July 1988. Bernie is now a depot driver in the train care depot. (*Andy Beavis*)

(*right*) Driver Fred Beavis, in the cab, with driver Ted Thornton. Fred was a friendly driver to go with and had a clever wit. He has retired but both his sons Andy and Jonathan are still drivers at Salisbury. Ted, now retired, was late for work one day; he was to have signed on at 02:00. As he left his house he walked down his front garden path and bumped into a donkey that he did not see in the dark. The donkey refused to move from the gateway, effectively trapping Ted, as a large hedge surrounded his garden. Finally after nearly an hour of pushing and nudging (the neighbours were getting a bit restless too) Ted finally escaped. (*Andy Beavis*)

4472 *Flying Scotsman* at Gillingham on 16 July 1988 with Fred Beavis in charge and Bernie Shergold as his fireman. (*Andy Beavis*)

A true image of Salisbury with the Cathedral spire in the background. Crompton 33053 was of the type of locomotive Salisbury drivers learnt as basic traction after steam, and is seen here in September 1977 approaching Skew Bridge with typical Mark 2 coaching stock. To the right can be seen driver Ted Noakes's allotment, which produced some very large carrots! The allotments are long overgrown, the up outer home signal above the second coach has gone and the bridge itself has been rebuilt, so this view is no longer available but thankfully *The Halfway House* pub still survives today and is now a free house. (*Pete Warren*)

Tom Doel

South West Trains 'on train' cleaner from Gillingham

Next are a few recollections from Tom Doel, one of Salisbury's finest storytellers, a very good model engineer, and not a bad train driver either! Tom started on the railways at Eastleigh in 1956 but a life change took him to Canada. In 1962 he was back working on the railways, this time at Salisbury where he worked his way up from cleaner to mainline fireman only for Salisbury shed to close with the end of steam. Tom made the decision to move away to get his driving job rather than wait and hope. He went to Maidstone and worked on the electric units of the Southern and returned to Salisbury in1985 on a redundancy move. Unfortunately for Tom he had to leave the railway with a serious medical problem in 1996. Thankfully he recovered and a year later was back on the railway again as one of the South West Trains group of travelling 'on train' cleaners working between Salisbury and Exeter. He is still working today and available for a chat anytime!

I remember once working with my driver Eric Cave on the afternoon Salisbury East Yard to Woking stone train. We had Standard 76007 and a full load of 27 grampus wagons; we left Salisbury and plodded slowly up the bank through Porton, our engine working hard. We were going slow enough that when we passed a Permanent Way gang round the corner between Porton and Grateley one of them shouted out: 'Got any coal for our hut?' I said: 'Not today, it's all a bit small. Bring you some tomorrow!' Next day we remembered to put a very large lump of coal on the footplate for the gang. Again we had a Standard, this time 76076, but our load was only 15 loaded grampus wagons so we made easier going up the bank. Sure enough, the gang were in the same place, we blew the whistle and they got ready to receive their delivery. I moved the lump of coal to the edge of the footplate and when we were level with them I shoved it out. Unfortunately, we were travelling faster than the day before and the lump of coal took on the characteristics of a bouncing bomb while we watched in horror as the gang dived into the hedges to avoid the coal. It hit one of the platelayer's pushbikes and sent it crashing through the door of the gangers' hut. We looked at each other and hoped no one was in the hut! When we signed on next day a message was waiting for us: 'Thanks for the coal, but we now need a new bike, door, table, kettle, teapot, cups and one window! No one hurt though.'

I was along with Eric one day during the big freeze of 1963 when the snow was lying deep everywhere. We took a GWR 2-8-0 up East Yard to work the cement empties over to Westbury. The shunter up the yard was Lance Lovett and he asked if he could have a lift home with us as he lived in Wylye. Eric said that would be OK. We set off with Lance on the footplate and he said: 'Just slow up at Wylye and I'll jump out' and Eric agreed. On the approach to Wylye, Eric duly started to slow up, aiming for the road crossing so that Lance could just step down off the cab steps onto the road. Lance, though, didn't want to go quite that far as his house was before the crossing across the field and said: 'Here will do fine'. Now we were still doing around about 20mph but before we knew it the crazy fool had jumped! I looked out but could see nothing but snow. Eric released the brake and opened the regulator and just said 'Idiot'. Next day we were on the same train and were relieved to see Lance at work. Eric said to him: 'What on earth were you thinking just jumping out like that?' Lance replied: 'It didn't look too fast, I ended up deep in the snow; it took me a good 20 minutes to get out! Can I have a lift today?' 'No way', said Eric!

Ron 'Rocket Ronnie' Luckins, looking out of the window, and Tom Doel seen about to work down to Yeovil with 4498 *Sir Nigel Gresley*. (*Andy Beavis*)

46229 *Duchess of Hamilton* runs into Salisbury past Marlborough Road footbridge under clear signals in November 1995. (*Paul Abbott*)

Nigel Scrivens

Network Rail Signal & Telegraph Department at Salisbury

We change departments now and hear from Nigel Scrivens who is still working at Salisbury but now has his own office.

A Signal & Telecoms probationer – the first day

Having been accepted as a probationer in the Signal & Telecommunications Department of British Rail at Salisbury I was told to report to the office in the station car park on Monday 4 September 1972 at 07:30. This seemed to me at 16 to be the middle of the night. I duly reported to Mr John McGuiness (Area Signalling Manager). Here I was issued with two pairs of blue bib & brace overalls, two blue jackets, one black Pee jacket and a set of oilcloth – yellow wet weather coat, leggings and hat. Also a tool kit, which comprised of an instrument screwdriver, a London pattern screwdriver, a pair of side cutters, a pair of pliers, 0Ba spanner, 2BA spanner and a penknife. I was then

shown the lineman's shop and was taken aback by the building. It consisted of an entrance door and paved brick flooring; in the right-hand corner there was a Belfast sink and two gas rings with a large aluminium kettle boiling away. A large table in the middle of the room was flanked by two trestle benches and at the far end a coke stove. The ceiling was open rafters, soot covered and hung with cobwebs. I was later to learn that the building had originally been for the storage of the horse-drawn fire tender. I was then introduced to the linemen who were Norman Maggs, Charlie Presslee, Reg Eynon, Mick Price, Dave Bevis and Bill Hatcher.

I was made welcome with a cup of tea. I was soon to learn that tea was an important part of the job and being proficient in the making of tea was a priority for probationers. I was assigned to Reg Eynon and Bill Hatcher who took me to Salisbury West signalbox

Seen in Salisbury East box in 1978 are (on the left) signal and telegraph technician Nigel Scrivens, who now has his own office, and Mick Price, the then area lineman, now deceased. (*Mick Price collection*)

signalbox to show me the signalling system; here I met the signalman and yet another cup of tea. From West Box I was taken to 'C' box which was situated at the entrance to the former Great Western station, an impressive building three storeys high. After another cup of tea I was taken onto the locking level which was undergoing alterations by the locker fitter and his assistant: Dave Ottaway and Paul Cosens, who had the nicknames of Boo Boo and Bonkers – to this day I do not know why.

The signalling in Salisbury in 1972 was far from being cutting-edge technology. It had semaphore signals and points operated by compressed air with 'C' box being mostly mechanical. Much of the week consisted of cleaning and oiling the points, rod runs and signals which involved large pots of paraffin mixed with oil for cleaning the point fittings. This was wiped off with cotton waste which, once saturated, was set alight, leaving small piles of burning waste around the yard. I soon realised that as a lineman you were very much in control of your own district, a very responsible and trusted position.

Signal & Telegraph staff in 1994.

Back row, from left to right: Mark Down (technical officer Salisbury), Paul 'Bonkers' Cosens (retired), Steve Dudman (technical officer Salisbury), Jim Wood (now at Basingstoke) Paul Brewer (now manager for Colas projects), and Brian Dowell (retired).

Front row, from left to right: Simon Pethick (now signal section manager, Eastleigh), Mick Lazarus (retired), Derek Russell (retired) and Mick Price (deceased). (*Mick Price collection*)

34060 *25 Squadron* has just attached to its stock in the carriage road and will now work the 4.00pm Salisbury to Waterloo on 12 December 1964. 34060 was a Nine Elms loco at the time and will end up at its home shed for servicing later. The tracks to the right are the GWR lines out to Wilton. Steve Anderson is the fireman looking out; the photo was taken by his friend Geoff Rebbeck.

(*right*) T9 30304, a Salisbury engine, has just come off shed to work a stopping service to Portsmouth. It will now shunt west over to the carriage roads to pick up its stock, which were situated between the SR and GWR running lines next to Salisbury West box (to the right of the water tower seen in the photo). The photo is believed to be have been taken in 1955. (*Mick Price collection*)

53809 in Salisbury Fisherton Yard before working a railtour on 26 September 1987. This is now where the Traincare Depot's berthing sidings are. (*Paul Abbott*)

46

Mike Wareham

Driver at Salisbury

Mike Wareham retired in 2005 after 49 years service; here are some of his thoughts.

I left school and was looking to become an electrician but could not find any work. My dad Stanley (better known to everyone as Sam) suggested working on the railways. He was already working in Salisbury steam shed on the coal stage, a job he took when he left the RAF after the war. My brother Jim was also a fireman at Salisbury so it was not too difficult to get an interview and I joined them working on the railways on 13 August 1956.

I started, like all the others, as a call boy, moving up to cleaner and eventually to fireman. I can remember going to the firing school down in an old coach body in the old down carriage sidings at Exeter Central. I spent a week there under the guidance of instructor Edgar Snow and each evening would catch the 16.30 train back to Salisbury, gaining valuable experience thanks to driver Ken Young and his fireman Doc Allen who were the crew working that train back. They let me have a go and by the end of the week I was able to quite impress Mr Snow!

One day I was with driver Ron 'Tigger' Pearce and we were coming back from Westbury with the Avonmouth loaded coal train with a WR 6300 loco. Coming up Westbury bank the engine was having to work hard to get the load up the incline and I was shovelling like a good 'un, when all of a sudden I thought something was not right. I turned to speak to 'Tigger' but he wasn't there! The WR engines never had any chains across the cab entrance and I thought, oh no he's fallen off! I desperately looked back, not knowing whether to stop or keep going as I knew that if I stopped we would never get going again. I leaned out so far looking back I nearly fell off myself. Starting to panic I turned round to look out the other side only to find 'Tigger' sat on the other side seat smiling at me with his customary pipe hanging out the side of his mouth. Somehow, without me noticing, he had walked round the front of the engine on the running plate and got back in on the opposite side!

I was along with Dennis Smith back in 1963 when we had all the snow, over at Westbury again; this time we had a GWR 2-8-0 and were on shed. Understandably, Dennis did not want to come back tender-first so he wanted to turn the engine on the turntable. All advised against this, including me, as Westbury's table was manually operated and I knew I would not be able to push it round due to so much snow, but Dennis insisted; so, it was to be. Sure enough, less than half way round and we had built up enough snow that I could not push against it; nor could it go round the other way, as it would just pile up again. We were stuck, until about two hours later and a lot of shovelling by a very helpful Westbury fireman and myself. We eventually got hooked onto our freight train and were on our way, slowly making our way up the bank until, just after Dilton Marsh, we hit a snow drift that our loco could not overcome!

Our guard that day was a Westbury man who must have only been days away from retiring, he looked so old! It was therefore left to me to walk back down the bank to find a telephone and get assistance. Luckily not

Salisbury driver Ron 'Tigger' Pearce seen with his trusty pipe. 35028 *Clan Line* was stabled in platform 5 at Salisbury during the steam specials of 1988. (*Andy Beavis*)

47

The view from Salisbury West signalbox looking out over West Yard. This yard was used for down trains and could cope with 250 wagons a day. Salisbury East Yard, which dealt with up trains and traffic to Southampton, Portsmouth and the south coast, could handle 560 a day. During World War II Salisbury was an extremely busy place; the traffic increased in West Yard to 600 wagons a day and in East Yard to 1,000, with the run-up to D-Day seeing 1,200 a day. (*Pete Warren*)

too far down the bank there was a small water pump house, which I knew had a phone in it. The trouble was it was down the embankment but I thought it worth the risk of not being able to get back up, so slid down, right past the pump house and hit the bottom fence post! After a frantic scramble back up to the pump house you could say I was not best pleased to find the door locked. Damn!

I managed to get back up to the running rails easier than I expected and just in time, as I heard a train coming down the bank so, without thinking, I waved my red flag to stop the train to get a lift. This train had Salisbury driver Jock Bell with an Eastleigh crew on a loaded petrol train. The resulting screeching of brakes, clanging of wagons and verbal expletives informed me that maybe I shouldn't have stopped them! I got the lift, just, into Westbury and came back up the bank with our

rescue engine, a Hymek diesel. I managed to warm up slightly before getting down and hooking the Hymek to the rear of our train. I told the Westbury driver: 'When you hear us blow the whistle we'll be ready to go'. I got back onto our 2-8-0 only to find Dennis had let the fire go out! It took another 40 minutes for me to get it going and Dennis would not blow the whistle till he felt he had enough steam. We eventually made it back and signed off, making 15 hours! Dennis smiled and said: 'That's a result, eh!'. I then realised!

One day I was working with Mike Wareham as his secondman on a late turn down to Exeter and back on a Saturday evening, and he allowed me to bring my girlfriend June along with us. She thoroughly enjoyed the trip and despite what Mike says, that was not the reason she married me!

Mike Wareham is seen getting off 4472 *Flying Scotsman* to make the tea. (*Andy Beavis*)

Paul Brighten

Station operative at Tisbury

Next up Paul Brighten who as you will see has been around a bit!

Summary of my railway career in and around Salisbury

Summer 1961
I left Gillingham (Dorset) School and after an interview at the British Railways Southern Region District Traffic Superintendent's Office at Exeter Central was appointed into a temporary trainee position. I had asked if I could work at Salisbury, but there were no vacancies.

1961-1962
My BSA Bantam got me to Gillingham for my first day at work. This was at 9.00am on Monday 3 October 1961 when aged 16. I started at Gillingham as Junior Clerk Class 4. In those days the training school was in London and considered far too far to travel, so all training was at my first-ever home station. My first attempts at the station accountancy gave rise to some unusual results and the booking clerk in despair once said: 'You'll never make a booking clerk'. It could be that even now, the PAC thinks no change there, then.

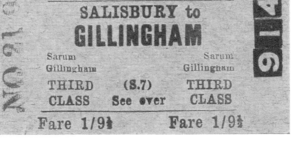

Gillingham's 26 staff worked under the watchful eye of the Stationmaster, Mr G.R. Sampson, who was in charge of the Booking Office (Ticket Office), Goods Office, Parcels Office, signalbox and a small fleet of five delivery vehicles. The station also had a cricket team and a skittles team. The station was gas lit, with the exception of the booking office which was lit by electricity. Tickets were issued using the Edmondson date press and the trains were all steam hauled; I remember being told that although diesels had been trialled in the 1950s, it was thought that they were too expensive to run and wouldn't catch on. The omnibus telephone system was amazing.

After a period learning all clerical duties in the booking, goods and parcels offices, I was by then 17 and became a temporary relief clerk working at Gillingham and also at Crewkerne (goods, parcels and booking offices), Martock, Semley, Sherborne, Templecombe (booking office and railway telephone switchboard), Tisbury, Yeovil Hendford Goods (I wasn't to set foot on Yeovil Junction station again until 1991). My biggest disappointment was that I was not allowed to go and work at Padstow and Wadebridge in the summer of 1962, because I was considered too young to 'lodge away'.

1963-1965
Early in 1963 the big freeze took hold and this made the railway, including the S&D, very busy as most roads were impassable and the train was almost the only mode of transport still going. At Gillingham many tickets were sold to local stations on the S&D via Templecombe for journeys that were only a few miles by road. Also in 1963 control of the Southern Region line west of Salisbury was transferred to the Western Region. I was on the Western Region for about a week. Shortly after the freeze and then 18, I left Dorset to work in the Booking Office at Kingston on Thames; boy was that an eye opener? Later I moved to Malden Manor on the Chessington branch and then to Surbiton. Once I had learnt the way things worked in the smoke, I also covered booking offices at a great number of stations in the London area.

1965-1966
I decided that I wanted to return to Dorset, so left the railway for just seven months to be an assistant transport Manager for Hine Quarries at Gillingham, but missed being on the railway.

1966-1968
Salisbury at last! Aged 19 and in my opinion very experienced and ready to take on the world, if not the universe; appointed to a clerical position at Salisbury Milford Goods Office. The people there were great, but the job itself really very boring, so transferred to the Shipping Traffic Freight Office at Southampton Docks, which I really enjoyed.

1968-1982

Two years later I made a transfer to Surbiton Enquiry Office (Travel Centre) and then received a promotion in 1970 to the Wimbledon Divisional Manager's Office at its out-based Salisbury office, where with Mr A.W. (Bert) Hunt, we planned, ordered and implemented the new ticket issuing arrangements (Bellmatics) for the old Edmondson card tickets for most of the south-western division stations. In 1980 Tisbury and Gillingham were transferred back from the Western Region, and Warminster went back to the Western Region. As both regions had a different ticketing system with different types of ticket and machine, this meant changing the Gillingham machine with Warminster's and starting completely from scratch at Tisbury.

1982-1989

In 1982 the Southern Region changed over to Local Area Management in line with the other four British Rail regions. The Divisional Manager's Office was set to close eventually and I was displaced. In October 1982 I was appointed to the position of 'first and last' Area Administration & Personnel Manager in the first (of the three to date) Salisbury Areas. Out of the 13 Southern Region Areas,

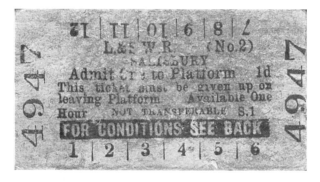

Salisbury was the smallest and most cost-effective; it outlasted quite a few until 1989, with practically no change of staff. A well-known saying evolved: 'There are two ways of doing things, the Salisbury Way or the Wrong Way'.

Salisbury's first ever Area Manager, Gerald Daniels, was a very experienced railwayman, who was responsible for numerous improvements, including the Laverstock curve and the Tisbury loop. He is well remembered for bringing back steam operation to the Salisbury Area, with some very innovative train operations between Templecombe & Yeovil Junction. With others, I was heavily involved in the campaign to reopen Templecombe station on 3 October 1983 and the Salisbury Area Special Events Team (1985-1988), which arose from the marketing to promote Templecombe. However all good things come to an end and the Salisbury Area was amalgamated with Portsmouth and Southampton in 1989.

1989-1991

For two years I was Head of Section Customer Services at Southampton and became heavily involved in setting up the Information Production Unit which produces pocket timetables and posters – a very interesting position, which saw the start of producing timetables with data downloaded from the timetable database.

1991-1996

Another boundary change came when the lines west of Templecombe and from Yeovil Pen Mill to Maiden Newton were transferred. This meant that the Station Manager at Salisbury needed another person to assist him with the extended area and I became the first SM to be based at Yeovil since the 1960s. This was the first time I had set foot on Yeovil Junction station, apart from changing trains for connections to Yeovil Town, Hendford Halt & Martock in my temporary relief days.

Following the introduction of the Area Retail Manager's (ARM) organisation at Salisbury (the second Salisbury Area), which was responsible for the line from Basingstoke to Pinhoe, I became the Area Ticket Office Manager (ATOM), based once again at Salisbury. A further change saw me back as Station Manager at Yeovil until November 1996, when I left the railway industry and the Salisbury area for the last time; or so I thought at the time.

1997-2009

Following a telephone call, 14 August 1997 found me back on the railway, this time in a part-time job at Yeovil Pen Mill working for Wales & West. Then, following another telephone call about 18 months later, 9 February 1999 found me back in the Salisbury patch at Tisbury.

Apart from eight months' secondment from June 2005 to February 2006 in connection with the introduction of the current STAR ticketing system, I've remained at Tisbury since 1999; this has been one of the longest periods of my career based at one location.

(*above*) Gresley V2 2-6-2 60896 of Doncaster is seen at Salisbury during the locomotive exchanges of 1948. (*Mick Price collection*)

(*below*) 45216 of Liverpool Bank Hall depot at Salisbury during the 1948 exchanges. (*Mick Price collection*)

Steve Anderson and Geoff Rebbeck

Drivers at Salisbury

Steve Anderson started on the railways in September 1961 and Geoff Rebbeck joined in April 1962. They were cleaners together and have remained friends ever since. Both are still drivers at Salisbury today.

When signing on as a cleaner you would go to the booking-on point and pick up a little brass disc, which had Southern Railways and a number on it, which was your number and was a simple way of clocking in and out as you had to hand the disc in to go home. The cleaner's shifts were from 6.00am till 2.00pm and 2.00pm till 10.00pm. In a shift you would usually clean two engines; the equipment you were given was a pair of plastic goggles to work the 'Weaver', a handkerchief to tie over your mouth, and your hat on back to front! At 15 years old you were also in charge of a potentially dangerous piece of equipment, the Weaver, a primitive steam cleaning device. This was a paraffin-fired, highly dangerous, portable steam generator that produced steam at pressure (caustic soda was also in the mix!) to blast off dirt and grease from the rods, motion, pistons and axle boxes. It was an art in itself to get the machine fired up and was usually done by dangling a burning rag inside, soaked in paraffin. Most of the cleaning of an engine was done using a cloth soaked in a mixture of oil and paraffin and hard graft. The rags were known as 'rustys' and were performing their last duties. They started as 'white ones', clean and soft, and were handed out to drivers when they signed on. At the end of the driver's shift he would hand them back in, they were washed and then given out to firemen who used to keep them a bit longer, but they would come back in, be washed again and now handed out to the cleaners; by now the cloths were a rusty brown colour and quite rough!

A cleaner would have a bucket full of rustys, and use them three at a time, one used for cleaning, the other two tied round each wrist to stop the oil and paraffin from going up their sleeves. Most days there would be impromptu Rusty fights where the cleaners threw heavily soaked cloths at each other; you knew when you were hit as not only did they hurt, they deposited there oily mess all over you and mother would not be best pleased at the extra cleaning! When cleaning an engine you had to get used to the dangers of each class. The S15s were notable in that when cleaning along the boiler on the driver's side you would be holding on to the handrail but this would cease to be a handrail near the front and became a red hot steam pipe! Naturally you would let go; at best you would get covered in oil at worst fall to the ground.

Looking every bit a 60's icon Salisbury driver Geoff Rebbeck is seen when he was a cleaner down the steam shed in 1962. (*Steve Anderson*)

When starting, first of all you were, of course, subject to all the usual tricks (or bullying as it would be called now) where you would be sent to the stores for a long weight, a bucket of sealed steam to start the loco, red paraffin for the tail lamp. Now of course the stores people were in on the act, but one practice had thankfully been stopped by the time we started and that was the use of graphite grease for ball greasing which used to take months to wash out, you can guess from where! You would be asked to go into the firebox to clean it out and then the door would be shut behind you and roped shut and you would be stuck in there until someone else heard your shouting!

One operation that used to spread panic if you were in the wrong place was when the loco was to have a blow down, an operation using full steam pressure and boiling water to flush out muck from the boiler with the steam; the water and muck were blown out underneath, and although the steam was coming out below, if you were in the cab you would have a job to breathe and the heat was tremendous. It was the quickest way to get rid of blackhead spots on your face as they would burst and be cleaned at the same time! The operation was meant to be carried out on the move between Porton and Salisbury Tunnel Junction but with the West Country and Merchant Navy class locomotives there was always a risk of the blow down valve sticking open which would mean you would lose all your water and have to chuck your fire out, and of course suffer the indignity of being pulled home by an assisting engine. So it was decided to put a blow down pit in on the line just before the coal road, but Bill Boyd, who was the blow down man, would do it in the shed, where he was not meant to. He would get on the loco, blow the whistle a couple of times and bellow out the side 'BLOW DOWN'. Everyone would try and get out of the shed, as the steam would fill the building like a thick fog. Sometimes locos were blown down on the coal road and if you were underneath raking out the ash pans and you heard a hiss, you moved out as quick as you could. Mind you, most of the time it would be either the sanders being checked or someone having a whiz on the hot clinker which would leave an awful smell and which would waft down the pit like a quiet assassin and grab your throat, yuk!

The cleaners' room was only small and there could be up to 20 young lads in there who were all fair game for the firemen to pull tricks on, and the stove was attacked many times; bicycle pumps full with paraffin were often poked round the door and squirted onto the red hot stove, the resulting flare removing many a young man's exposed hair; thick oil would be poured down the chimney and the room would be blacked out for hours as the smoke would be so heavy you almost had to brush it out the door. Ted Noakes covered the chimney one day and nailed the cabin door shut. The screams of panic were heard for miles!

Geoff – The Warships had hydraulic transmission with gears and they used to make a lot of noise and be a bit rough riding especially at first change at 15mph, then again at 30mph, but into top at 40mph they were not so bad, but of course it would all happen again when coming down the gears; they always seemed to be more alive than any of the other diesels and you had to take more care when drinking a cup of tea!

Steve Anderson is seen driving an unknown Warship diesel. Most Salisbury men did not have a very high opinion of the Warships; they were rough riding at high speed, the cabs would get excessively hot due to the transmissions and they were unreliable, but probably it was just because they replaced the West Countrys. (*Steve Anderson*)

They also had so many buttons and warning lights that to a young lad it was like flying a space rocket. One day I was on one and the back engine shut down (Warship diesels had two engines) so my driver told me to go back and check the engine: 'Don't touch the transmission trip button, sonny', said my driver sternly but with a slight worried tone. I went back and could see nothing wrong with the engine, but the transmission trip button was just too much of a temptation and before I knew it I had pressed it. I don't know why, I just had to! The engine was then flung into gear and there was a horrible sound of crunching gears, so I pressed it again and all went quiet. I went back to the cab and said: 'Couldn't see anything amiss'. My driver turned his head slowly, looked at me and calmly said: 'You touched that button, didn't you?' We carried on in silence to Exeter on the one engine with our fingers tightly crossed!

D819 *Goliath* standing in platform 1 after working a stopping train up from Yeovil, in October 1964. This Warship was one of the few that had its multiple working capabilities reinstated. New on 25 April 1960 it was withdrawn on 3 October 1971 and was cut up at Swindon on 3 March 1972. (*Pete Warren*)

Salisbury drivers Eric Judd (on the left) and Ted Noakes in a pose that you can make your own captions up for! Eric, who has retired, loved to tell you a story, which we didn't mind as to tell it you would have to do the driving as Eric would forget what he was talking about otherwise! Ted, another who has sadly passed away, was one of Salisbury's top pranksters. He was as strong as an ox with hands the size of shovels and an excellent engineman. (*Robin Coles*)

Area Manager
British Rail
South Western Road
SALISBURY, Wiltshire, SP2 7RS
Tel: 0722-29600

Mr S Anderson
Driver
SALISBURY

Dear Steve

BLACKMORE VALE EXPRESS — SATURDAY AND SUNDAY 9TH/10TH JULY

You are no doubt aware of the immense enjoyment and satisfaction you have given to our 200 customers on each day travelling on the Yeovil services and I am writing to not only confirm this but to inform that you that it is my great pleasure to present you with a Service Excellence Award for your stirling efforts on the footplate.

The circumstances are well known to us both and the understanding with the train recordists and enthusiasts is such now that occasional excesses are treated with discretion.

You are therefore cordially invited to our next Awards Evening in early August on a date yet to be fixed and I will let you know as soon as possible.

Meanwhile for a superb performance; it has further enhanced the public image of our Salisbury steam event.

With kindest regards.

G Daniels
Area Manager

The closest you will get to to being congratulated for speeding on the railways! I can't possibly comment on the alleged speed. (*Steve Anderson*)

Steve Anderson is seen cleaning 60532 *Blue Peter* in August 1966. Driver Ron Page is walking up to get on her and take the loco off shed if Steve's done a good enough job! (*Steve Anderson*)

Wendy Hillier

Passenger to Waterloo for 30 years

Having become part of the furniture after 30 years of commuting between Salisbury and Waterloo I was asked if I would like to contribute something for this publication; how about my most memorable journey? Well, apart from the evening a bit of the engine flew past the window; the morning I was locked in the loo because the hydraulic fluid froze; the time the brakes jammed and caught fire; or the Beaujolais Nouveau parties, it's got to be the Season Ticket Holders' Forum on 4 June 1985.

Gerald Daniels, Area Manager at that time, somehow hijacked a couple of Orient Express carriages complete with chefs and waiters and hooked them on to the back of the 07.42 Salisbury to Waterloo train and sent out the invitations. I don't remember much about the Forum, possibly because it was in the other carriage,

Gerald Daniels, Area Manager Salisbury, is pleased to welcome you aboard the Pullman Cars of the Venice Simplon-Orient-Express for the Season Ticket Holders' Forum, which will be held during the journey to London this morning.

Tuesday 4th June 1985

MENU

07.42 SALISBURY-WATERLOO
4th June 1985

Fresh Orange Juice and Champagne

Fresh Melon, Grapes and Grapefruit

Scrambled Egg Garnished with
Crispy Bacon and Chives

Smoked Sausage, Mushrooms, and Saute Potatoes

Rolls, Croissants
Butter and Preserves

Coffee from Colombia
or Tea

†Drawing from original menu 1884.

but the breakfast was something else. Melon, scrambled egg, bacon, sausage, mushrooms, croissants, with enough Bucks Fizz to render us paralytic by Basingstoke – I think the pitchers became 99% orange juice after that but it was too late!

The luxury of the carriages was unbelievable with comfortable armchairs (essential after Basingstoke!), fresh flowers on the tables, real soap and towels in the loo, etc., etc. Sadly, it seems that I'm the only one left who remembers this momentous occasion. It was great PR – any hope of a repeat?

I am glad that Wendy enjoyed her breakfast. I too can remember the day as it was I who attached the two Pullman cars carefully onto the rear of Wendy's train.

BREAKFAST 9 / –

Plain Breakfast 5/- (excluding main courses)

_____

CHOICE OF :—

Fruit Juice   Stewed Fruit

Porridge

Shredded Wheat   Cornflakes

_____

CHOICE OF :—

Grilled Fresh Fish

Kippers

Bacon & Egg

Bacon & Sausage

Sausage & Egg

_____

Grilled Tomatoes   Sauté Potatoes

Preserves

Toast   Rolls

Tea or Coffee

John Quinlan on his first day working the restaurant car on the Atlantic Coast Express, where he served the breakfast shown on the menu (*right*). He would work right through to Padstow, returning the next day. John recalls the T9s that worked the ACE into Padstow or Bude from Okehampton; they romped along with only four coaches on. John's daughter Sarah is now a guard at Salisbury. (*John Quinlan collection*)

An unidentified GWR Hall approaching Salisbury at Skew Bridge on the GWR route. This location is now an overgrown mess. (*Malcolm Lewis*)

Charlie Davies

Guard at Salisbury

Charlie Davies is currently Salisbury's most senior guard with 39 years' service. Here he remembers two tales from his early days.

I started on 31 March 1970 at Salisbury as an office boy taking notices around the station and signalboxes. I then got promoted to railman working on the platforms; one day I was given a greyhound and a pigeon in a cardboard box to take from platform 2 to platform 6 for the Portsmouth stopper service. The greyhound had come up from Gillingham and was going to Poole to be raced and the pigeon from Exeter was to be released from Southampton. The greyhound was raring to go and pulled me along all the way to the Portsmouth train formed of a 3-car Hampshire unit that had a small guard's van. I put the box down and went to put the dog's chain through the securing loop to tie him up. When I pulled the chain through the loop it stopped short; I looked round to see what it was stuck on but it wasn't stuck. The dog had gone over and put his head in the box; I pulled sharply on the chain which pulled the dog out just in time to watch it gulp the pigeon down in two quick bites! I took the box to the Station Manager and showed him the only remains – a couple of feathers. He looked at me and told me to be more careful, his face contorted somewhat as he tried not to laugh!

In 1973 I got my guard's job and soon after I was booked on a ballast job on a night turn and had to go by taxi to Warminster and relieve my train at 23.00. To get to it, though, I had to walk off the end of the platform towards Salisbury, the train being just out of sight past the overbridge. It had been raining most of the day but, thankfully, had stopped although there was a lot of surface water and puddles. The gangers had been doing a fair bit of digging out of the chalky ground with the down line totally lifted. I had to walk along on the sleepers of the up road. We are taught from day one to walk ballast to ballast as sleepers can be slippery, I had not gone far when I found out that this advice was vital as I slipped on a sleeper and fell straight into one very large, white, watery patch of chalky sludge. I felt both my outstretched arms sinking further into the quagmire and I was starting to blow bubbles in the white water! Amongst all the gurgling and squelching sounds there was another noise; a chorus of laughter from all the gangers! I pulled my self out and was covered from head to foot and looked like a ghost! Eric Moores, the guard I was to relieve, had seen me fall and once he to had stopped laughing kindly pulled my hat out of the mix – it was stuck peak first in the ground!

It was only my pride that was hurt. I had to carry on and work like that all night; how the job got done I don't know as everyone was just falling about laughing on seeing me! When I got back to Salisbury at the end of my shift an audience had assembled to witness the railway's first walking ghost!

1058 *Western Nobleman* was used on a down train because of flooding at Gillingham, being able to work through deeper water because of its hydraulic transmission. 1058 was new on 25 March 1963 and withdrawn on 24 January 1977, having covered 1,312,000 miles. In a comparable time a class 159 unit would have covered over 2,500,000 miles. (*Pete Warren*)

Every now and then things do not go quite to plan; the next three pages offer a selection of photographs showing a variety of mishaps!

(*right*) Due to a wagon hotbox, the up Meldon to Woking stone train derailed at Dinton but the train carried on with just one axle off the road for a further two miles until Barford curve where at the time the track was old bullhead 60-foot length rail. The combination of curve and track brought about the resulting mess! Salisbury driver Ken 'Smokey' Shergold was at the controls but no blame was attributed to him. (*Andy Beavis*)

(*left*) A Grampus wagon was to blame for the derailment. The wagons in this photo ended up being left at the site for some time after, as they were clear of the running line, and were eventually cut up there. 1 June 1980. (*John Hill Jnr.*)

(*right*) In October 1973, whilst running around a train of box wagons, the shunter and crew got their angles messed up and did not have as much room as they thought, nudging one wagon over. The Eastleigh breakdown crane is just about to lift the stricken van. (*John Hill Jnr.*)

(*left*) An 08 shunter is rerailed by the Eastleigh breakdown crane outside the GWR Salisbury 'C' box in Fisherton Yard in April 1972. This box controlled the entrance to the old GWR terminus station and goods yard. (*Pete Warren*)

Whilst Salisbury steam shed was being cleared during 1968 Fratton driver Pete Brown brought in a DMU to stable there until its return working. Unfortunately, the rails had got covered with oil and grease and as he applied the brakes the unit started to slip and went through the wall into the driver's mess room where 13 men were enjoying a cup of tea. Luckily most escaped without injury except for Harry Gibbons who was taken to hospital and tragically had to have his foot amputated. The wall was propped up but never repaired as there were only months to go before its demolition. Seen facing the camera, from left to right, are Keith Noble (he became a driver at Salisbury and retired early in 2008); Willy Wiltshire (he became and still is a driver at Salisbury); Roy Goodfellow (a driver at Salisbury, now retired); Barry Symons (he moved away to get his driving job in 1967 but returned to Salisbury in 1980 and is now retired); Brian Lucas (he moved away for a driving job at Waterloo in 1975 and is now retired). (*Steve Anderson collection, by permission of* The Salisbury Journal)

(*left*) About 15 minutes before departure of the 16:15 Salisbury to Waterloo on 12 July 1986 driver Steve Anderson noticed the engine 33103 was low on coolant water so the whole train was shunted over to the holding sidings next to platform 5 where the engine received a quick top up of water. The shunter that day was Barry Yeatman. When they had finished he positioned himself in the cab of 33103 and Steve drove from the 4-TC unit. Barry informed Steve that they had the signal, which they did, into West Carriage Sidings but unfortunately they did not have the ground signal at the far end. Barry noticed too late and despite applying the emergency brake the train ran through the catch points. The 16:15 did not run that day! (*Barry Yeatman*)

(*right*) In 1973 a Bristol to Portsmouth DMU was derailed by a set of faulty points with the result that the front car went one way and the second tried going another. Seen looking at the damage is Reg Eyon, standing closest to the DMU; he was the Signal & Telegraph linesman. Bent over is Ron Evans, linesman's mate; watching with the long blonde hair was Barry Mansbridge, an S&T probationer. (*Nigel Scrivens*)

(*left*) 33112 *Templecombe* at Eastleigh after a collision at Salisbury which buckled its chassis and frame, resulting in the loco's withdrawal from service. (*John Hill Jnr.*)

Salisbury had one very bad day when on the night of 1 July 1906 the Plymouth to Waterloo boat train crashed at the east end of the station.

Rivalry and being seen to be the fastest were key traits of train companies in the late 19th and early 20th centuries in their goal to achieve commercial success, particularly where journeys were offered between the same or similar points by different companies. With the GWR and the LSWR both serving Plymouth by different routes to either Paddington or Waterloo in London, passengers arriving by steam ship from America were viewed as a lucrative market. Each company was keen to win the majority of the available revenue without conceding anything to its rival.

During 1903 the LSWR ran American Ocean Liner specials when required and these were operated on a regular, weekly timetabled basis from 9 April 1904. Although there was a gentleman's agreement that the GWR would handle the postal mail and the LSWR would deal with the passengers, the pursuit of the fastest journey between Plymouth and the capital continued by both companies.

Shortly after 02.40 on Sunday 1 July 1906 the LSWR train, drawn by L12 locomotive No.421, approached Salisbury at a minimum of 60mph despite a permanent speed restriction of 30mph applying to the curve at the London end of the station. The restriction was because of a complex scissors junction on this curve. As the train rounded the curve, the engine, due to its high centre of gravity, leant over and struck a milk train coming from the London direction on another track. The resulting crash, according to the *Salisbury Times*, reverberated across the city and resulted in the loss of 28 lives which included 24 of the 43 passengers who had joined the train from the liner SS *New York*, mostly Americans, along with the driver and fireman of the express, the guard of the milk train and the fireman of another train.

Salisbury has come close to disaster on two other occasions, both during the Second World War. The first was when a rogue German bomber flew over the city during the day, a story I have had related to me by several people. First my Dad, Roy Pearce, who was still at school at the time, says: 'I was on the top deck of a bus going down Fisherton Street into town when I saw the plane flying low past us. It then started to turn and went out of sight but came back round and went low over the bus, heading back towards the railway station. I knew it would try and bomb the steam shed and I got

very worried, as my Dad and brother Ron were both at work there. I jumped off the bus and ran as fast as I could back to the steam shed to see what was happening.'

Meanwhile my Mum June can also recall the bomber: 'It flew right over the railway goods yard and over our house and then turned to come back. I was in the back garden and mother shouted to me to come in and get under the stairs but before I could the bomber was overhead and I heard a squeal as its bomb dropped. I fell to the floor and covered my head. There was an almighty bang, everything shuddered and windows broke as the bomb hit two houses nearby in Donaldson Road but we were OK.'

Bob Bailey recalls being told about the incident by several drivers when he started. 'They told me the bomber came in very low from the station towards the shed and let its bomb go; thankfully as he was so low the bomb had a fair bit of forward motion and hit the metal bridge pillars of Ashfield Road which are curved making the bomb 'bounce' enough that it went over the steam shed and landed in the allotments in Cherry Orchard Lane and exploded there.' *In the mess room at the time were my Grandad and Uncle Ron. Ron said*: 'We were sat having a cup of tea when we heard the plane go over and then a huge explosion and what sounded like machine-gun fire that turned out to be just all the mud and shrapnel falling on the shed!' *As I mentioned, my Dad was running to the shed*: 'I heard two explosions and feared the worst. When I finally arrived at the steam shed I was very relieved to see both Dad and Ron stood with several other staff in Cherry Orchard Lane looking at the damage. The large water tank above the shed buildings was covered with mud splatters and dents from shrapnel. Ron told me the only real damage was to the allotment which, ironically, belonged to the shed foreman Bert Miller!' *Actually not only did the railway have a lucky escape but so did I!*

Salisbury's second brush with disaster is a story we have been told over the years at work. During the war Salisbury's West and East yards handled a huge amount of War Department traffic and daily trains of aerial bombs passed through the station. One evening when there was particularly heavy armaments traffic there came an air raid warning, with many planes droning overhead. In platform 4 was a train of over 40 wagons of ammunition, standing on platform 2 a special train of bombs and nearly 500 soldiers, in platform 1 a special ambulance train and in West Yard were 35 wagons of bombs. The warning lasted a considerable time; to the staff and Station Master it seemed like an eternity. The bombers certainly missed an opportunity to do some serious damage that night!

Robin Coles

Former Driver at Salisbury

Let's get back to the stories and hear from Robin who started on the footplate a couple of months before me. He is now a driver at Exeter but we have remained good friends.

I have so far worked on the railway for 35 years, most of which has been on the footplate. I come from a long line of railwaymen, most working for all or part of their service in and around Salisbury. My great grandfather, Thomas H. Coles, was working in 1871 as a pointsman, he later went on to become a guard on the LSWR at Salisbury. His son, my grandfather, Thomas Coles, started as a telegraph messenger in May 1891. He went on the footplate in Salisbury on 27 August 1895; in 1907 he moved to Exmouth Junction depot near Exeter to get his driving job until 1910, returning then to Salisbury. My grandfather finished his time in the old man's link on day turns going to Bournemouth via West Moors and also Portsmouth Harbour via Southampton and Eastleigh. Whilst in this link, he was known to be involved in the odd deal with naval sailors wishing to exchange surplus cigarettes, which in turn would then be available at cost to railway staff at Salisbury. He retired in 1945 aged 65.

I started working at Salisbury Station in 1970, whilst still at school. After school and at weekends I would go to the station to set up a small table in the booking hall to sell newspapers along with Charlie Davis. We also had to walk up and down the platform selling newspapers to people on the trains, calling out the name of the paper; many times the money and the papers were exchanged through open windows as the train started to pull out of the station. This would not be allowed today in our safety conscious railway and definitely not by schoolchildren for pocket money. At quiet times between trains we used to play football down in the subway whilst we were supposed to be working.

It was during this time that I started to take an interest in the trains themselves. When I left school, I tried to get a job on the railway with the Signal & Telegraph Department (S&T) but failed the exam. In May 1973 I reapplied, this time as a messenger at the station, at the rate of a journey railwayman on £11.30 per week. The job was to work for the Station Manager, Mr Owen Faisey and his relief manager John Smith. Frank Asher was the chief clerk who gave us most of our jobs. These included sorting and taking notices to all the signalboxes, station and yard staff. I had to make tea when asked by the office staff, especially when anyone important turned up to see the Station Manager. I also accompanied one of the managers on Thursdays, on the pay run by car to all the staff outbased at station and signalboxes, all boxes to Warminster, Andover and Romsey. I used to enjoy this part of the job as it got me out of the office for a day. I was never sure why I went out on the runs unless it was to act as an extra pair of eyes as they had a lot of money on them at the start with the wages for all the staff. I shared this job with Charlie Davis (now Salisbury's most senior guard), Peter Pearce (the second most senior guard at Salisbury), Paul Locke (who went on to become a carriage and wagon fitter for over 20 years before leaving to become a fireman with the MoD fire brigade at Boscombe Down airfield), David Franks (now managing director of National Express Group trains division) and Gary Pollard (now a driver at Salisbury).

In March 1974 I was transferred to the job of traction trainee, which was at the bottom of the driving grade. This job started with a course at Southampton training school where we were taught how to read signals, hook up locomotives and the dangers of moving trains and live electric rails. After this I returned to Salisbury taking up the role of secondman, which involved riding with various drivers from Salisbury and other depots on a variety of locomotives and units to a number of different locations. Exeter, Waterloo, Portsmouth and Bristol were the main routes. Occasionally a pilot driver would be present and we would go further still to places like Cardiff, Newton Abbot and Bognor Regis. At times I would be called to other depots such as Southampton Docks, Basingstoke or even Waterloo, making these days extremely long.

During the mid 1970s the class 33s made up the vast majority of the work. These locos were noisy and rough riding at speed; however, they were reliable and clean. One of my memories with these locos was to see driver Alfie Smith mending watches at high speed whilst he was being pitched and thrown around while I was doing the driving. Other types of locos that we worked on at the time were the class 08 and 09 shunting locos; on the odd occasion the drivers would leave us secondmen to do the shunting while they went to get their hair cut or go to the market, even sometimes the bookies. Now

(*above*) Driver Thomas Coles with King Arthur class loco 754 *The Green Knight* at Exmouth Junction just before working back to Salisbury in 1933. Driver Coles had just worked down to Exeter with 757 *Earl of Mount Edgecumbe* with 12 coaches (412 tons) in a record time of 87¾ minutes. (*Robin Coles collection*)

(*below*) Thomas Coles seen with N15 King Arthur class 1413 on Salisbury shed which at the time was her home shed in 1939. He was driver Robin Coles's grandfather. (*Robin Coles collection*)

and then we would also get class 31s and 47s to drive, adding to the variety. The Thumper Units (Hampshires) were used on stopping trains to Portsmouth and Reading, but on Saturdays a 12-car set of these units used to run from Brighton to Exeter. Very often on this run one or more of the four engines would shut down en route and the secondman at station stops would have to go and get water in a bucket to top up the engine. In 1974 I worked on one of these units with driver Ken 'Smokey' Shergold to Bridport via Yeovil, the last ever rail tour to work over the branch before closure two weeks later.

The class 50 locomotives began arriving in Salisbury in June 1980 for crew training for use on the Waterloo service. These locos were powerful and very fast at pulling away, so much so that occasionally guards giving the green flag on platforms would get left behind, especially at Honiton where the platform was deep and on a severe curve! The guard would then have to follow the train in a taxi to Feniton to catch up with the train. Some of the work around this time included freight; with this there was a variety of cargo comprising of oil trains to Fawley Oil Refinery where any cigarettes, lighters and matches had to be handed in on arrival and reclaimed on departure because of the potential fire risk. Another cargo where caution was needed was working ammunition trains. One evening whilst trying to pick up a train load of live explosives from Dean Hill MoD, bound for the Falklands War, the key holder for the gate could not be found so the gate had to be cut off its hinges due to the urgency to get the explosives to the boat awaiting departure at Southampton Docks. Armed

guards accompanied this train. We worked newspaper trains at this time from Waterloo. On arrival at Andover, the driver and secondman would assist in unloading the newspapers in exchange for a bundle of papers. After leaving Andover we would travel over a viaduct under which driver Bernard Shergold lived. We would tie a newspaper with string to a large stone and drop the paper off the viaduct into his back garden as we drove by; he would pick up the paper later, sometimes finding it in his greenhouse!

In January 1980 I started my training course at Stewarts Lane, London to become a driver. The course lasted six months and was attended by drivers from across the Southern Region. During this course we were taught rules and regulations, the mechanical workings of the locomotive and basic route learning. At the end of this course I was then qualified as a driver. However this did not lead to a permanent driver's job because we had to wait for the older drivers to retire.

During 1981 my wife and I bought our first house, a small terrace house originally built for railwaymen in Churchfields Road, opposite the station. We lived so close to the station we could hear all the announcements from the platforms. Every morning we would be woken at 6:30am with the noise of an engine being started outside our house; this engine would then carry on running until it moved at 7:15am. Despite this, the location of the house was ideal for me to stop my train nearby to offload items to be collected later. On one such occasion this was helpful when we were landscaping our garden and building a rockery. On a number of trips to the stone

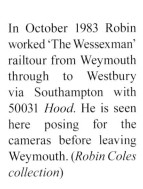

In October 1983 Robin worked 'The Wessexman' railtour from Weymouth through to Westbury via Southampton with 50031 *Hood*. He is seen here posing for the cameras before leaving Weymouth. (*Robin Coles collection*)

quarry at Whatley in Somerset I would fill the back cab with large rocks, stopping outside our house to deposit them. Also collected and deposited were Christmas trees in December from the embankment near Grateley, which involved taking a saw to work. During our trips to Exeter we would order 56lb bags of potatoes from the station staff at Honiton who knew the local farmers and on our return we would pick up the potatoes, placing them into the guard's van and bring them back to Salisbury. On some night turns we would stop and pick mushrooms from farmers' fields; on one occasion we were spotted by the farmer who chased us back to our train.

One of the turns disliked by the drivers at Salisbury during this time was the late shift on a Saturday, especially if you had to pass the British Railways Social Club, catching a glimpse of the other drivers enjoying themselves on a night out with their family and friends. To make matters worse many of the partygoers would gesture their glasses at the train as you went by.

In the mid 1980s coaches for exhibition trains were prepared on the site where the depot is now. These were companies wishing to advertise their products or services; these trains would then travel around the country, such as the *Daily Mirror* newspaper and the Welsh Tourist Board. In September 1983 it was decided to send a class 25 loco to Salisbury to be repainted to match with some coaches. The locomotive was sent from Bristol on a Portsmouth service; however, at Salisbury, Albert Cooke, the foreman on duty, refused

to swap the loco with one of his class 33s, as none of the Salisbury drivers were trained to drive class 25s, therefore the loco with the Bristol driver working it had to continue on to Portsmouth and then back to Bristol. It was sent back the following day light engine from Bristol to Salisbury. That day it was unofficially started and driven up and down the yard by a number of the secondmen and drivers, myself included. The steam heating boiler was also started. The engine never did get painted as it was decided it was not suitable; it then left Salisbury to be scrapped.

Driver Only Operation turns were implemented on empty stock and freight trains. Known as D.O.O. shifts, working without a secondman or guard, the driver was paid an extra £7.32 per trip in the 1980s. Another bonus was paid when drivers worked over 200 miles in a single day's turn. Due to this, turns to Waterloo and Exeter paying an extra £33 were the preserve of the top link only drivers! Payday was on a Friday, with the pay office located on platform one; a line would be formed and in turn cash in hand was given after showing your pay card with staff number plus name.

By March 1985 I was still a passed secondman with no promotion imminent at Salisbury. My wife and I decided to move to get my driving job. We moved to Walsall, West Midlands in June 1985 where I took up a driving job at Bescot. We stayed there until April 1992 when we moved to East Devon, having been transferred to Exeter St David's depot where I remain a driver today.

Tallyllyn Railway's narrow-gauge loco *Sir Haydon* is being prepared for a journey with the Welsh Tourist Board's exhibition train from Salisbury to Birmingham International in 1984. Driver Ted Noakes, who worked the train as far as Reading West, looks eager to have a drive of the little engine. (*Colin Hall*)

Porton Station

... and a number of apologies from Gary Pollard, now a driver at Salisbury.

I was born at Porton and grew up there, living within sight and only a five-minute walk from the station. Porton station was similar in size and design to other nearby village stations, for example Wilton South and Dinton. Living so close to the station and liking my toy trains it was inevitable that I would go and watch the trains. It was the early to mid 1960s and steam trains were still running. On a late summer's day I would make my way over the footbridge to the down side of the station and head towards the London end of the platform, climb the bank, crawl through the fence and scrump some delicious plums from the small orchard by the brick bridge (that is still there today). Once my 'haul' had been gathered, I took it to the footbridge, sat down on the bridge cross-legged, and started to devour the plums. To dispose of the evidence of my 'steal' I dropped the plum stones down the chimneys of any steam engine that would pass under the bridge. I remember one day standing on the platform when a train stopped. I went up to the engine and stood in awe at the size of the wheels and the valve gear with all the steam hissing out. Then the engine whistle blew and the train started to move. What a noise, I just watched in wonder as this huge beast made its way slowly out of the station and gradually disappeared in the distance on its way to Salisbury.

A young chap called Barry Lake worked at the station and if he was on duty I would hang around and make myself a nuisance to him. There was a phone on the wall inside the booking hall and to use it each station had a Morse-like code: 3-2 for example. When one station called another the appropriate code would be tapped out and if you heard your code the call would be for your station. I had watched the staff carefully and learnt the code, and would wait until Barry was occupied, usually as he sat down to start his tea, and then crawl along the booking office floor, hidden by the counter, and tap in the code for Porton station. I then lay in wait to watch. Barry came to the phone, picked it up, said 'Hello, hello' but with no reply he would replace the receiver and return to whatever he was doing. I would then do it all again but usually on the second or third time he would cotton on to what was happening at which time I would make a hasty retreat in fits of laughter.

Despite all the childish games my friends and I made against the staff they were all very friendly and would often invite us to help out on the station. Come dusk I would stand outside the lamp hut, opposite the station house, and wait for whoever was on duty until they came to the hut to light the Tilley lamps. These were used to light the station at night and my favourite job was to place the lamps on their brackets on the footbridge – I felt so important. The most exciting moment was when I got to walk up the track carrying the freshly trimmed and topped up lamp for the 'Down Home' signal. I waited at the bottom of the signalpost while the member of staff climbed up and replaced the lamp; I got to carry the old one back.

On the last day the station was open I took the opportunity to travel with my mother to Salisbury by train. I think my ticket cost sixpence and the engine was a Warship class. This was a treat, my first time on a diesel-hauled train. My family normally travelled to Salisbury by bus and we wondered why they shut the station!

I would like to apologise to Ren Judd, a retired driver of Salisbury, for it was his plums that we would scrump; to the firemen of Salisbury shed (I still work with some of them) for the plum stones in your smokebox. Last but not least, to the staff of Porton station, c.1963 to closure, especially Barry Lake, for putting up with the antics of the village boys. I am sure we put you through hell.

Let's hope they all forgive you Gary!

Salisbury driver Ren Judd is about to start preparing 34077 *603 Squadron*, a Nine Elms engine, before taking her off shed to work the 4.00pm Salisbury to Waterloo in May 1963, unaware his plums were being scrumped! (*Steve Anderson*)

Paul Abbott

Driver at Salisbury

Now we hear from someone who did not know what was behind the motive power entrance doors.

I joined British Rail straight from school at the end of June 1981, no hanging around on street corners for me, I wanted to earn some money. I had always had an interest in railways although I didn't spend much of my life loitering on the station with my notebook and flask. I believe it is possible to have railways in the blood as my great grandfather William had started his railway career on the Somerset & Dorset as a wheeltapper and later joined the London and South Western as assistant examiner at Milford (Salisbury) among many other locations. My grandfather Percy was a driver at Salisbury. I also had two uncles on the railway at the time I joined, Norman & Arthur Abbott, who were drivers at Salisbury.

There weren't actually any vacancies at the time but within a few months the messenger, Mark Salmon, would be leaving the Station Manager's Office (SMO). The only way the Station Manager at the time, Mr Owen Faisey, could employ me was by the Youth Opportunities Scheme (YOPs) that had recently been started by the Government and it turned out I was one of the first to join BR Southern Region via this scheme. The plan was that while on YOPs I would be able to train in a variety of railway roles and then be ready to take over from Mark in the SMO when he moved on. For the first few weeks I worked with Mark learning the messenger's role. In the days before email and Lotus notes the messenger was vital in passing messages and post from HQ between departments. The major plus side to this was that you got to know everybody in every department; you couldn't ask for a better grounding and experience.

At that time at Salisbury there were the Permanent Way offices in the first floor East block, the Exhibition Trains offices in the GWR Goods Shed, the Motive Power Department in the first floor West block offices (although NOBODY was allowed in there it seemed). The Carriage & Wagon Department was on platforms 1 and 3 and finally the electricians (two of them, nicknamed 'Positive' and 'Negative') were based in a room in the station subway. In the 80s all Ticket Office staff, station staff, guards, signalmen and crossing keepers reported directly to the Station Manager, collectively known as the Traffic Department. There must have been at least a hundred staff in the Traffic Department alone. Also

under control of the SM were the signalboxes at Wilton South and Salisbury Tunnel Junction.

After working with Mark (he was counting the days until his appointment to a guard's position) I worked in the Red Star office, regularly working on the left luggage counter, another element of railway life long since forgotten. Otherwise I spent my days assisting the station staff on the platform or the carriage cleaners who worked on platform 5 or platform 1. In those days there was no carriage washer, the work was done with a stiff brush and a bucket; a thankless task, particularly in the middle of winter.

It was then decided that for a few weeks I should experience life at some country stations. Although I did wonder if the SM wanted to get me away from the influence of some of the station staff (you know who you are!) I did a few uneventful weeks at Tisbury with Terry Fower and then a week at Gillingham. Now you could say the platform staff at Gillingham were a bunch of characters with the two Eric's, Messrs Smart and England, and Clive Webb, 'Roger' to those who remember him. This was a proper country station with, it seemed, an 'under the counter' trade in coal, bacon and sausages. An odd mixture you may think, but as there was a coal merchant and a meat factory in the station yard that would probably explain it! Phone orders came in from all over the South Western for bacon, sausages or a bag of coal, which were duly packed and despatched on the next available service, payment usually sent via the guard. At the time I was just happy to be working for my £27 a week.

In January 1982 Mark was released to take up his position as guard at Salisbury and I was called to start work in the SMO on 4 January 1982, finally a full-time member of BR staff, and with a £5 a week pay rise to boot. First job (and I've always been told the most important) was unlocking the office at 8.00am and putting the kettle on for the arrival of the Station Manager; Assistant Station Manager John Smith, later Gordon Dudman; chief clerk Frank Asher; and guards' roster clerk John Carpenter who all arrived around 8.15 to a fresh cup of tea. Next I met the train from London at 8.35, quite often with a 'brute' (a large wire cage on wheels for moving post or parcels either pulled manually or towed behind a tractor) to collect all the post for Salisbury and out locations under the SM's control. This

Railman Paul Abbott in 1984. Paul is now a driver at Salisbury. (*Paul Abbott collection*)

would often include posters, boxes of working notices and letters. By the time the postman had called you had a huge pile to sort into stations and departments; you then spent the rest of the morning on deliveries. After a few weeks I had this worked out and was regularly sitting in East or West box with the signalman by 11.00, after I had made his tea, of course! If there were no special duties then all was quiet until 15.00ish when the return post was collected for distribution back to HQ, etc. So I then had to return to all the offices picking up their post which (for HQ) had to be sorted and put on the 16.20 to Waterloo. The one exception to this rule was the Motive Power Department; for some reason they always brought their post down to me at the end of the day. As I said earlier, I never got inside the door, let alone into the offices.

My day was over at 16.30 but I regularly did a few minutes unpaid overtime assisting the ticket collector on the barrier as the 16.39 to Exeter was regularly packed with girls from the local Technical College and I always did my bit to ensure they got to their train safely! After six months as messenger I was told I was too old to remain a junior railman (the post had a maximum age limit of 18) and I had to move onto the platform as a railman. I had come full circle and soon found myself training my replacement, Graham Hansford.

It was a sad day when I left the SMO; money aside it is still the best job I have done during my railway career. Since then I have worked in ticket offices, telephone enquiry offices, administration offices, also meeting my wife Jane along the way. In 1998 I got my current position as a driver at Salisbury, so I did finally make it into the MPD!

Salisbury guard Peter Pearce seen with a very tatty looking flag about to leave Exeter Central with a Waterloo train on 9 April 1979. (*Robin Coles*)

25069 leaving Salisbury on a Portsmouth to Cardiff service on 19 August 1983. The engine was booked to come off the train at Salisbury but as no Salisbury drivers were trained on the class 25s, Albert Cooke, the running foreman that day, would not swap one of our class 33s for something he could not use! (*Pete Warren*)

Working the 10:10 Exeter St David to Waterloo on 21 February 1979 were Salisbury driver Francis 'Bim' Dables and guard Don Robb. Bim was a keen photographer and was employed by most of us as our wedding photographer. Bim would always send his secondman to the chip shop at Exeter to get fish and chips with country pie twice and of course whatever you wanted! Don would have been the ideal guard for Bim as he would very often bring in copious amounts of eggs, bacon, sausages and tomatoes and cook breakfast for whoever wanted it. (*Robin Coles*)

(*below*) On Friday 10 June 1983, 46026 *Leicestershire and Derbyshire Yeomanry* worked the 11:30 Meldon quarry to Salisbury East Yard. It is seen in the reception road where Salisbury driver Robin Coles piloted the Exeter crew (ex-Exmouth junction driver Den Vosper and secondman Neil Cannon) up to East Yard and back down into the holding sidings. The Exeter crew had their break and then returned 46026 to Exeter on the 16:38 departure from Salisbury along with train engine 33015. (*Robin Coles*)

Salisbury driver Eric Jenkins about to work back with a loaded stone train from Whatley Quarry on 3 May 1979. Eric was a very placid man, I never heard him argue or indeed swear, very unusual as most sentences on the railway are twice as long as they need be, simply because of one word! (*Robin Coles*)

(*below*) An interesting photo taken from 35006 *Peninsular and Oriental S.N.Co.* as it backs into Salisbury's platform 5 to work a stopping train to Yeovil, after coming off the shed, which can be seen in the distance. Salisbury West signalbox can also be seen. The concrete cabin to the right was shelter for the firemen who were given the job of shovelling down the coal and watering the down trains that arrived in platform 4. Above this cabin and in the distance can been seen the Southern Region's stationery distribution centre (with two doors, one of which had rail access) that in turn stood where the GWR shed had been situated. (*Mick Foster*)

Annie Winter

British Rail's first woman driver

Next we hear from someone who started a real culture change in the footplate grade.

It was a passing thought that would usually have been forgotten before the day was out, but this one I remembered and it changed the course of my life forever.

I was out of work after handing in my notice at the Surrey veterinary practice where I had worked for three years after leaving college and I was sitting at Clapham Junction station waiting for a train to Victoria where I was going to meet a group of friends. The train arrived with the driving cab directly in front of me and I wondered whether a woman could be a train driver. Later that day I asked the question of one of my friends who was at the time working as a signaller at Aylesbury and, although he didn't know the answer, he gave me the contact details of the South Western Division of the Southern Region based in Worple Road, Wimbledon. Next morning I rang the offices and asked if it was possible for a woman to be a train driver. The girl who answered my call laughed so much that she was unable to speak so a man took the phone from her and, in answer to my question, said he didn't see why not although it hadn't been done before. He advised me to apply direct to a London depot which I did.

On 6 August 1979, days after a politically incorrect interview during which three senior managers questioned my plans for marriage and children and whether I had heavy periods that caused me to take time off work, I arrived in the Depot Manager's office at Victoria for my first day as a traction trainee – what was then the first step in line of promotion for the driving grade. I was handed a large brown paper bag which contained all the publications, keys and equipment I would need and I was introduced to a chubby 16-year-old boy 'runner' who had been sent to conduct me to my new depot and who could not have been more embarrassed at the task he had been given. Neither of us realised it then, but this was to be the first step in a process which would see me passed out as Britain's first woman train driver just 3½ years later.

The next few years were a culture shock for me and, as somebody with no railway background (I came from a BBC family), it was a very steep learning curve. The railway is like a parallel universe with all its traditions, ingrained practices and slang, and for an outsider like me it was a lot to take in. Hearing the older drivers' tales of how they had come up the hard way 'through the steam' and how long they had had to wait to get their jobs as drivers, I was surprised that they didn't seem to feel any resentment at how quickly by comparison the younger trainees could progress through the grades.

I was second manning in 'civvies' for many months as my requests for a uniform were turned down on the basis that I would probably leave to get married. This came to a head when I was working a football train with a senior driver of rather military bearing who was incensed when a policeman on the platform at Kensington Olympia came up to ask him a question from some of the football fans on the train who wanted to know what he was doing with his 'bit of stuff' in the cab. On our return to Norwood the driver informed the foreman that he would not work with me again until I had a uniform. As if by magic, a uniform was delivered to my home by special delivery the following week!

Norwood Junction was a wonderful depot for a driver's assistant as it had a wide variety of work and routes but after nearly three years I applied for a transfer to Waterloo as it was easier to travel to and from home and also because the grade progression was faster there. As soon as I arrived at Waterloo I was notified that a place was available for me at the South Side Training School and on a warm August Monday I reported there to begin the intensive six months of driver training, known as MP12. This was an exciting but worrying time. The end of my training was in sight but I had done all my early training on diesel locomotives and now my final driver training period was to be on electric multiple units (EMUs). Our instructors stressed that although things we had to learn might be hard to grasp at the start everything would fall into place as the course progressed. He was right, but I went through Christmas that year wondering whether things would fall into place before or after my final exams.

I was so nervous I barely slept the nights before my exam days but I needn't have worried as everything went really well. Our examiner stressed that he would be treating me exactly the same as my male counterpart (we were examined in pairs) and to be honest I don't know who was the more nervous, my male colleague or I. The three days whizzed by and the final part of my exam was to drive a train from Effingham Junction to Waterloo in the late afternoon of Thursday 17 February 1983. There was some slight confusion in the cab due to me talking to the train (I still do it). The booked driver of the train we had requisitioned stayed in the cab talking to my examiner and as we left every station I urged the train on as I opened up the power controller. My examiner thought I was talking to him and asked the booked driver who was standing between us 'What did she say?' to which he starchily replied 'Come on, sausage'.

After shutting down the cab on arrival at Waterloo I was asked the final question of the exam: 'Do you feel ready to take on, on your own?' I had already been warned that however nervous I was feeling it was important to reply with a confident 'Yes' to this one and when I did so my examiner told me that I had passed for driving and he gave me my EP key and a pair of regulation sunglasses and told me to report back to my depot the next day. I left the cab feeling as if I was walking on air.

AT THE HELM — fulfilment of a four-year ambition for former veterinary nurse Anne Winter.

Southern's First Lady takes to rails

BRITISH RAIL'S first woman driver proudly reported for duty at Waterloo today.

Anne Winter, 23, from Surrey, is the the first woman in the BR network to study and pass the intensive three-year drivers' training course.

Her ambition to break into that most male-dominated of professions began in 1979 as a daydream at Clapham Junction.

"I had been unemployed for a few weeks and was sitting waiting for a friend at the station. I watched a train pull out and thought: 'I'd like to drive one of those,' she said.

"The first British Rail person I spoke to about it was at Wimbledon Station and she just laughed. But eventually they realised I was serious.

After three years as a driver's assistant at Norwood Junction she transferred to the training school at Waterloo, passing the course com-

REPORT : Neil Darbyshire
PICTURE : Mike Lawn

had her final medical—the last formality.

Most of her male colleagues have treated her well. But she knows that all eyes will be on her when she starts driving for real.

Jokes

She said: "While I was training there were the usual jokes like 'the train standing at platform one will be delayed as the driver has a broken fingernail' but it was mostly in fun.

"I'm not really frightened about starting to drive, but I know that everyone will be watching and there will be some just waiting for my first mistake."

Trains, however, were not Anne's first love. Until she was 19, she worked for three years

It is quite a career leap to looking after pekes and poodles to being responsible for up to 1000 peak-hour commuters.

"I suppose it is," said Anne. "But I don't look on it like that. I have always been interested in mechanical things and like messing about with old cars as well."

Anne, who is single and lives with her parents, was not always interested in trains and went into her present job "on pure impulse".

She said: "I have always been interested in machines and my ambition is to be a good train driver.

"It doesn't matter whether you are a woman or a man as long as you can do the job well."

Anne also owns two old cars

is devoted to their preservation. She is a member of a classic car club for Morris Oxfords and Austin Cambridges.

Before becoming a fully-fledged driver, Anne will have to spend about six months learning the routes on Southern Region's South Western service.

Colin Marshall, a former teacher at the drivers' training school, said: "She will have to learn about braking distances and gradients on the routes before becoming a relief driver herself. But she passed the course fairly easily. So she should do fairly well.

"There has never been any bar to women becoming drivers. It is just that none wanted to enter the course. That is changing now and there are five women training at the moment."

He added: "Some of the men will be a bit funny about them to start with, but I am sure they will get used

A new set of terrors awaited me on Tuesday 22 March 2009 when I was told to book on at 09.00 and report to the Press Office at Waterloo to face the media. The day rushed by in a flurry of questions and orders to 'Stand there', 'Sit here', 'Smile', 'Wave', 'Walk down the platform', etc., as the newspaper, television and radio journalists got their claws into me. By the end of the day I was exhausted but it was fun to see myself on the evening news on TV and hear my interviews on the radio later that day.

The 'Male Chauvinist Pigs' in our midst regularly made themselves known to me when I was going about my duties in the early years, including a city worker on his way home in the early hours of the morning.

Sporting a bowler hat and umbrella, he made his way to the front of the train and asked if I was the driver of the train. When I confirmed that I was, he replied that in that case he wouldn't be travelling, which amused me as he would have a three-hour wait until his next service.

On another occasion on a very hot day I had my Personal Needs Break at Strawberry Hill and I decided to get an ice cream as I walked to the station to relieve my next train. When the train came in I was still eating the ice cream and as I passed the driver I was relieving (who looked close to retiring age) he muttered 'F****g hell, I never thought I'd be relieved by a bird sucking a lollipop'.

Things have certainly changed over the years and nowadays if people have negative views on women driving trains they tend to keep these to themselves but over 25 years since I first passed for driving trains I'm still amazed at how often passengers express surprise at seeing a woman driving a train. Perhaps, we should be promoting train driving as a career choice to schoolgirls otherwise in another 25 years we might not have moved much further forward.

It's impossible to condense memories of 30 years' railway experience into a short piece like this. I could fill a book with stories of my years on the railway so, who knows, perhaps a new career awaits me in my retirement?

This piece is dedicated to the memory of Brian Hawes – driver and gentleman

Editor's Note: Annie moved to Salisbury Depot in 1991.

Annie certainly blazed a trail for women drivers. As mentioned earlier we now have 8 female drivers at Salisbury and also 13 female guards; all are part of everyday railway life, and it is no surprise to us.

Annie Winter is seen leaning out of the cab of 159003 *Templecombe*. Alongside, from left to right, are Bob Lawrence, her guard for the day; Norman 'The Foreman' Henstridge who was the train crew supervisor (retired April 2008); Michael Hughes, porter, who was retiring on this day; Keith Usher, driver standards manager (ex-driver, now operations manager); and Adrian Roper, ticket office clerk (now a driver). (*Annie Winter collection*)

Tom Hatcher

Driver at Salisbury

We now go back a few years and hear from someone who started their railway career on the other side.

When I was a child we lived in No.13 Windsor Road, Salisbury where, next to the house, there was a large arch that led through to a yard with a stable block for horses that the GWR used for their delivery carts. The horses themselves came by train from Bristol where they normally worked extremely hard, coming to Salisbury for a rest! I can remember coming home from school and sitting on the wall in Windsor Road so that I could watch the trains shunting in Fisherton Yard. I was seven at the time and my Dad, Thomas Henry Hatcher, was a fireman at Salisbury GWR shed and if he was on the pannier tank that did the shunting they would come up No.1 road next to the wall and let me get on the footplate. I would spend the next hour shunting the yard with them. I even got to throw coal on the fire and try and drive but I did not have the strength to open the regulator! Then I would go home, have a wash and go to bed. I was destined to work on the railways. On the GWR when it was your turn for promotion you were expected to take the next vacancy that came up within the company and because of this my Dad twice worked away from Salisbury, having a spell at the centre of the GWR at Swindon until he then moved to Pontypool Road.

I left school at 14 and my Dad had put my name down to work on the railway but I could not start for the GWR until I was 15, that was their rule, so I started working for Salisbury Printing Company at their press in Wilton Road, mostly making the large posters for film releases. I had to leave there after only six months as the ink and chemicals brought me out in a bad rash. I then got a great job working for Cadbury's chocolate; they would send their chocolate by train and I would unload it and put it on the delivery cart and sometimes I got to go out with the delivery man. If any of the load was damaged it all had to be sent back; well, at least most of it was returned!

On 15 September 1941 I started on the railway at the GWR shed in Salisbury. I was actually 15 that June but there was no vacancy then so I had to wait till September. This delay meant that I would work on the railways for 49 years 9 months and would not get my 50-year badge! My first job was a call boy and I remember being out one night knocking up drivers. I had just woken up one

driver in Heath Road at 03.00; the next one was only down the road a little but not for another 40 minutes and it was raining so I went and quietly stood in somebody's porch and waited. Now when we were kids the bane of our life was a policeman called PC Askey as every time we did anything remotely wrong he would spring up out of the blue! I was once in Roman Road on my pushbike and went to give a girl a ride home to her house on the crossbar of my bike and we had gone no more than a couple of feet when we hear: 'Hello, what's going on here, then?' It was PC Askey. 'You know you shouldn't be doing that; where do you live as I need to tell your parents?' I told him and went straight home. I could not believe it; when I got home PC Askey was already there telling my Dad everything! Dad told me off too. Well, I am stood in the porch for no more than a minute when I hear: 'Hello, what's going on here, then?' It was PC Askey at 03.00 in the morning on his bike; how the hell did he do it! Did he ever go home? I explained what I was doing and he went on his way. I saw him from time to time, well he saw me, when I was knocking up and he would just say: 'Hello, my boy, knocking up?'

I was lucky that because of the war I soon got promoted to fireman, as there was so much extra work. I was also lucky that the next vacancy was at Salisbury! I can recall climbing to the top of the water tower on shed at midnight and looking right over to Southampton and seeing the flashes of the explosions from the air raids on the docks. We were lucky in Salisbury, the one time we did get bombed it only landed in the allotments by the SR steam shed.

We had about 50 sets of men at the GWR shed in four links, a passenger link, two goods links and the shunting link. We would go to Cardiff in the passenger link using one of our Halls, the two goods links involved going to Westbury or Bristol with the 2-8-0s and the shunting link was working in Fisherton yard shunting coal wagons, cattle wagons and general goods using pannier tanks. Salisbury was a sub-shed of Westbury and by the time I started, most of the engines we used were officially based at other depots but 6960, 6961 and 6966 were unofficially ours! I can remember on several occasions being with my regular driver Stuart Harris and racing the Southern crews out of Salisbury to Wilton as the tracks ran parallel to there. I think the honours were pretty even! Several of our drivers like Charlie

The GWR sheds at Salisbury. This is now an industrial site but roughly where the ground signal is sited in the foreground there is now the CET (toilet emptying facility) and emergency fuel point for the Salisbury train care depot. (*Danny Finnis collection*)

(*below*) Brush class 31 loco 5817 waits for the road into Salisbury in May 1972 as it works the Bristol to Portsmouth vans. It is standing on the GWR lines next to the site of the GWR steam shed that was the smaller building behind the third and fourth vans. The larger buildings were used from around 1958-1968 by the Southern Region as their stationery distribution depot. The site is now an industrial estate, but the rails are still in use as this is where the toilet emptying and emergency fuelling facilities and carriage washing plant for the train care depot are situated. (*Pete Warren*)

6997 *Bryn-Ivor Hall* comes on the GWR shed at Salisbury. (*Mick Price collection*)

Titt and Bert Griffen were in the home guard during the war and they would come to the shed at night for a cup of tea and sit down; the Germans should have invaded then as most of the others that were on duty at night would join them! On the GWR we had fire-droppers (they would prepare and dispose the engines). Most of the fire-droppers at Salisbury were Italian POWs and were bussed in from their camp at Alderbury. They were typical Italians, always after the women and a young couple lived opposite the shed in Ashfield Road. He was a pilot with the RAF and was away a lot, whilst she made the Italians happy!

When the GWR shed shut in 1950 about 30 men moved over to the Southern shed, me included. This was a bit of a culture shock for us as not only did we now have to prepare and dispose of our own engines but we had to fire on the right; the opposite to what we were used to. Some men never got the hang of it and left. The SR men were not happy with us coming over because it put many of them back as so many of our men were senior to them, but it all worked out over the years.

It was great to get the opportunity after 20 years to get back on the steam in 1988 when I was lucky enough to work on 6998 and a few others. I was surprised at how it all came flooding back and was so easy to drive, plus we did not have to prep or dispose the engine as each one had its own support crew, just like the good old days!

(*right, middle*) Tom Hatcher, on the right, felt at home, 20 years on, but fireman for the day, Steve Anderson, took a while to adjust to shovelling from the 'wrong' side on 6998 *Burton Agnes Hall*. (*Andy Beavis*)

(*right, below*) Tom meets an old friend at Bridgnorth, 6960 *Raveningham Hall,* which was a regular at Salisbury GWR shed. (*Tom Hatcher collection*)

(*above*) 'Tadpole' units were not regular visitors to Salisbury; 1204 is about to work the 15:15 Salisbury to Reading on Monday 19 May 1986. (*Colin Hall*)

(*below*) An unidentified Class 33 on an Exeter to Waterloo service passing the newly installed Wilton Junction in late 1972. Note the MoD aviation fuel delivery siding for Boscombe Down airfield, taken out of use on 18 January 1973. (*Colin Hall*)

(*above*) From left to right, driver Den Bentall, Traction Inspector Roy Porter and driver Richard 'Codge' Cottrell on Schools 828. All are now retired. Den was a great driver to go along with. He was always cheerful; if he was in a bad mood his smile was just not so big! Roy was a very fair inspector; he would give you a telling off if you deserved it and not expect you to do it again. Codge was another jolly man who would organise the rosters for everyone, presenting the list clerk with a 32-driver change of turns for the week. He still organises discos and horse racing games, raising lots of money for charity. (*Steve Anderson*)

Working back on the steam did funny things to some! Drivers Doug Harding (left), Pete Rebbeck (right) and Pete Truckle (in the rear). (*Andy Beavis*)

Tom Hatcher was a very good driver who never lost his temper; if he was upset or annoyed he would walk away, let the situation calm down and then come back. All secondmen liked working with Tom because of this and he encouraged us along the way when letting us have a drive. Most of the drivers at Salisbury would let you do at least half of the duties driving; it was how we learnt, from the best. Management knew this happened and trusted the driver's judgement. If you were no good then you didn't get to drive so we had to perform how each driver wanted us to, which had the advantage that we learnt many slightly different styles. When we went up to the training school on the driver's course that lasted six months we were taught driver's rules, traction knowledge and assessed on our driving skills by instructors Fred Johnson, Ted Lynch, Mick Oakley and Cyril Sweet, all ex-Salisbury firemen and drivers. We had to be good as we all wanted to be passed by the best! Salisbury still provides excellent instructors at the training centre, now with Gerry Bond, Chris Foot and Jez Morgan. For many years ex-Salisbury driver Roger Luckins was in charge of the training centre; he has only recently moved on and now works for the Rail Safety and Standards Board travelling around the world. We have provided the railway with many good managers: Keith Usher, Richard Davies, David Franks, John Hartford and John Penny to name but a few and next we hear from another one.

Garry Shaftoe

Local Operations Manager (Salisbury) for Network Rail

A summer's day in 1970 saw two bored schoolboys watching trains passing the signalbox at Codford level crossing on the line between Salisbury and Warminster. Sensing their enthusiasm for trains, the friendly signalman in the adjacent box invited them up to show them how the signals and crossing gates worked. So began the lifelong enthusiasm for railways and a lifelong friendship between the signalman, John Penny, and one of the boys – me! There followed many years of unofficial visits to various signalboxes in the Salisbury area that whetted my appetite to become a signalman myself when I was old enough.

Leaving school in 1976 I began work for Barclay's Bank and then the Civil Service before the lure of a career 'on the railway' proved too strong. After much encouragement and help from my friend John Penny I applied for a job. John was a relief signalman and it was he who arranged an interview for a signalman's vacancy with the Salisbury Station Manager, Owen Faisey, and his assistant Gordon Dudman. The interview seemed daunting to me at the time as both managers knew that there was a re-signalling scheme in the pipeline and that the signalbox was scheduled to close in a couple of years. They almost seemed to be trying to put me off becoming a signalman and to persuade me to consider a career in the ticket office instead! Strangely, one of the questions asked of me at the interview by Owen Faisey was 'did I like cabbage'? What relevance this had in the selection process I'll never know! Suffice to say, and despite my dislike for cabbage, I got the job as a Grade A signalman at Salisbury Tunnel Junction signalbox, entering service with British Rail on 17 September 1979.

Much of my first week on the railway was spent 'on the platform' at Salisbury station gaining an understanding of how the railway worked and an understanding of railways in general. Working mainly at the parcels office with Steve 'Ginger' Blackmore, Michael Hughes, and chargeman Maurice Osborne I spent hours unloading and loading parcels from trains, then taking them into the office ready for transfer onto the delivery lorries or onto shelves in the storeroom to await collection. General platform duties and cleaning of the station toilets also featured in my work. Fortunately, Mr Faisey sensed my enthusiasm to start learning my trade as a signalman and soon let me move out to Salisbury Tunnel Junction signalbox. The roster clerk, Frank Asher, kindly arranged that John Penny 'cover the vacancy at the tunnel' and, much to my delight, I was then able to commence learning the signalbox with John who had nurtured my interest in signalling all along.

I spent approximately two months working early, late and night turns whilst I waited for a place on the next signalman's course at Beckenham in Kent. The intense four-week course was to learn all about the theory of signalling trains using 'Absolute Block' and 'Track Circuit Block'. Successfully passing the course in December 1979 saw me return to my signalbox to gain more practical experience before I undertook a rules exam at Woking with the Area Movements Inspector, Bill Waylett. I then had to 'pass out' for the box by working the signalbox unaided under the close supervision of Mr Waylett. My first day as a fully qualified signalman marked John Penny's last day as a relief signalman for he then took up a promotional move to become one of the Station Supervisors at Salisbury.

As a fledgling signalman at Salisbury Tunnel Junction, I worked with the two other regular signalmen – Reg Flower (who was working on beyond normal retirement age until the box closed) and Rory Wilson. I also met many of the relief signalmen including Bob Blandford, John West, George Collins, Terry Fower, Harry Walton and John Morgan who 'covered' the box for annual leave and sickness. I gained useful experience as a signalman and always enjoyed watching the trains pass my tiny signalbox situated in a deep cutting in the 'v' of the junction just outside the mouth of Fisherton Tunnel.

As part of the first stage of the re-signalling in the Salisbury area, Dean box was closed in September 1980 and my box took over the signalling of trains between Salisbury Tunnel Junction and Dunbridge. This increased responsibility saw the box re-graded to become a Class B which, in turn, saw the two Salisbury boxes re-graded to Class C. Salisbury Tunnel Junction became a very interesting box to work as it now supervised the operation of the automatic level crossings at Dean and Dean Hill as well as the operation of ground frames at East Grimstead, Dean station and Dean Hill. Daily freight trains still served the military sidings at Dean Hill whilst a three-times-weekly trip freight from nearby Quidhampton served the chalk quarry at East Grimstead. Regulating these freight trains amongst the other passenger and freight

services often proved to be a real challenge. The main line to Waterloo also became more interesting with the introduction of faster class 50 locomotives that slowly took over the duties of the class 33 locomotives on the Waterloo to Exeter trains.

The summer of 1981 heralded the next stage of the Salisbury area re-signalling when new three-aspect, colour light signals were erected in the Tunnel Junction area and engineering work began on clearing the vegetation from the embankment and installing track which was to become the new 'Laverstock Loop'– a spur line linking the Waterloo and Southampton lines.

Monday 17 August 1981 was a sad day as I had the dubious distinction of closing Salisbury Tunnel Junction signalbox for the very last time. The new 'Salisbury panel' box, located in part of the old parcels office store-room on platform 4 at Salisbury station, took over control of the junction and the main line as far as Grateley, and the Southampton line as far as Dunbridge. After closing the box I made my way to the new 'Salisbury panel' to witness signalmen John Say and Derek Hopkins get to grips with the new push-button technology alongside Movements Inspector Fred Barrett from Bournemouth. The other two Salisbury boxes – Salisbury East and Salisbury West – closed in the same week, on Wednesday 19 and Friday 21 August respectively, with signalmen Ernie Foreman, Barry Lake, Albert Smith and Bob Blandford transferred into the new 'panel'. That week saw the last of the air-operated semaphore signals and points removed from the station to be replaced by modern three-aspect, colour light signals and hydraulic point machines – still in use today.

Salisbury Tunnel Junction signalbox which controlled the junction where the line from Waterloo and Basingstoke met the line from Eastleigh and South-ampton. (*Robin Coles*)

Fortunately for me a signalman's vacancy existed at Wylye signalbox, so I transferred there, working with signalmen Hubert Colbourne and John Morgan. This was to be only a short-term stay as this box also closed and control transferred to the Salisbury panel. Once again, I had the dubious distinction of closing the box for the last time on 26 April 1982. Within minutes of me sending the closing bell signals, the Salisbury technicians began stripping the box of its signalling equipment ready for the box to be demolished so that the new Automatic Half Barriers could be installed. With no more signalman's jobs available then I was employed as a hand signalman in the area as the re-signalling scheme progressed to the next stage which involved the closure of Codford signalbox and the manned level crossing at Upton Lovell. I did, however, manage to achieve one ambition by working one shift in Codford box as a signalman, before the box closed on 22 June 1982 – the very location where my interest in becoming a railwayman had originated.

Fate took a hand in my career at this point, for a regional boundary change took place that saw the management of Gillingham and Templecombe signalboxes and Tisbury Gates level crossing transfer from the Western Region to the Southern Region. This change resulted in the creation of two new relief signalman posts based at Gillingham. Despite having little 'seniority', I was lucky to be appointed as General Purpose Relief (GPR) signalman at Gillingham and so began my long association with the West of England line that continues to the present day. I spent three busy years as a relief signalman covering the signalmen at Gillingham and Templecombe and the resident crossing keeper, Sid Dunn, at 'Tisbury Gates'. Templecombe station re-opened in October 1983 so the Templecombe signalmen all received training in selling tickets, as part of that signalbox became the ticket office. This made the job at Templecombe very interesting and all the signalmen, including the two resident ones, Stan Flood and Ernie Day, rose to the 'retail' challenge very well, vying with each other as to who could sell a ticket to the furthest or most unusual destination!

In 1984 I was promoted to a Class D signalman at Salisbury 'panel' and spent four years operating the panel,

Garry Shaftoe in Wylye signalbox.

the passenger information system and also acting as the Salisbury station announcer. The job was a busy one as the East Yard was still in use for general freight traffic and as a hub for local freight services to Ludgershall and Marchwood whilst the East Carriage Sidings were used for the railway ballast traffic to and from Meldon and Whatley quarries. The former Fisherton Yard (now the site of the Salisbury Traincare Depot) was still used as a base for the British Rail exhibition trains. All trains were loco-hauled or formed of 'Hampshire' diesel multiple units so there was extensive shunting and 'running round' of trains at the station, requiring the assistance of shunting staff including Max Loadman, Brian Miles, John Carter, Brian Bone, Brian Tinham, Cyril 'Taffy' Jones, Roy Hooks and many more staff long since retired. Close working relationships also existed between the Salisbury signalmen and many of the 'platform staff' and Train Crew Supervisors including Maurice Osborne, George Raddon, John 'Lardy' Hill, Bert Vincent, Les Butler, Paul Vincent, Michael Hughes, Steve 'Ginger' Blackmore, Gareth Langford, Tony 'Moses' Gurd, Carlo Zacharelli, Maggie McDonald, Albert Cooke, Les Symes, Ken 'Dapper' Day and Dick 'Marko' Marks.

After four years my career took a radical change of direction when I was promoted to Relief Station Supervisor based at Southampton, covering the Station Supervisor's positions at Southampton and Bournemouth and the freight yard supervisor at Bevois Park near Southampton. A year later I became a Regulator (shift supervisor) at the Eastleigh Area Signalling Centre which brought me back once again into the signalling fraternity. Commuting from my Gillingham home each day was difficult and so I was pleased when I was able to transfer back to Salisbury in 1990 as a Duty Manager (Train Crew) working with Les Symes, Ken Day, Roger Long, Norman Henstridge and the 'non-clerical timekeepers' Basil Sergeant, Clive Munns, Bob Bailey and my good friend Danny Finnis. Working closely with the Salisbury-based drivers and guards was a new and challenging experience as I had very little experience of train crew conditions of service though they all helped me in my new role. The end was in sight for locomotive-hauled services on the West of England line as the increasingly unreliable class 47/7 locomotives made each day a challenge for the Salisbury duty managers to find enough serviceable locomotives to run the service. The introduction of the class 159 multiple units and the opening of the Salisbury Traincare Depot marked a notable change in the history of railways at Salisbury. The new trains were modern, clean and – most of all – reliable! The role of the duty manager became almost boring in comparison to the days of 'scavenging' and 'borrowing' locomotives to operate the train service.

Privatisation of the railways was looming, so once again I considered my future. If I stayed where I was I would be locked into the train crew side of the industry with little hope for future promotion. A chance arose for me to switch back to my signalling roots when I was offered the position of Relief Area Movements Inspector based at Eastleigh. This post provided cover for the Area Movement Inspectors (AMI) at Eastleigh, Salisbury and Bournemouth. Fortunately, I spent little time at Eastleigh, my time mainly being at Bournemouth and working with my old friend John Penny at Salisbury, now also an Area Movements Inspector. The first stage of privatisation saw me absorbed into the Railtrack organisation and following a company re-organisation into the role of Signal Manager for a two-year spell based at Bournemouth, managing the signallers (signalmen had become signallers) between Brockenhurst and Dorchester. Successive re-organisations saw my job title change to Signaller Manager and my office location fortunately move back to Salisbury. Railtrack became Network Rail, my job title changed again and I now became a Local Operations Manager managing the signallers, crossing keepers and railway operations at Salisbury, Gillingham, Templecombe, Sherborne and Yeovil Pen Mill. John Penny took up a similar role with me at Salisbury with responsibility for Yeovil Junction, Chard, Axminster, Honiton and Feniton.

In August 1992 the Salisbury signallers and I celebrated the 21st birthday of Salisbury 'panel'. We held a party where the signallers and maintenance staff, with many retired staff, gathered to reminisce over old times and recount amusing anecdotes about staff past and present. Signaller John Say featured, and continues to do so, in many of these amusing tales for he is the one remaining signaller from the original team of six still working as a signaller at Salisbury. John has played an important part in Salisbury signalling history having been involved in training every single signaller in the history of the Salisbury 'panel' box. John's experience of signalling trains at Salisbury is second to none!

My own 30-year career in the Salisbury area has been an interesting and enjoyable one as I continue to work with dedicated and experienced teams of railwaymen from all departments. Salisbury has an envied reputation in the rail industry where its staff work together with no 'barriers' or animosity between departments or companies of our privatised rail industry. We all work together (as in BR days) to provide a good service to the travelling public. Challenges are overcome in the 'Salisbury way' and nothing is ever too much trouble for the hard-working teams of signallers, train crew, station staff and maintenance staff from the Permanent Way and Signal & Telegraph teams.

Whenever rail staff, past or present, gather at Salisbury laughter is never far away – a sure sign of a happy and contented group of dedicated railwaymen who are proud of the tradition of being 'a railwayman at Salisbury'. Long may that tradition continue!

Salisbury 'C' box seen at the start of its demolition in early 1974. The box was opened in 1901 by the GWR to control their station complex; it was reduced to ground frame status on 27 October 1973 and closed completely on 2 December 1973. The site is now occupied by the shunters' cabin for the Traincare Depot. (*Pete Warren*)

Six-car DEMUs 1032 and 1034 working the Saturdays only Exeter St Davids to Brighton. This was a favourite turn for Salisbury men as it was doubled manned (the driver had no time for a break at Exeter); you would sign on around 11.00 down to Exeter and straight back to Salisbury by 16.30, nice and short! To the left of the picture is Fisherton Yard where exhibition coaches can be seen along with the coal yard and wagons. This area is now the Traincare Depot for the 159s. To the right are the two roads that were called the West Carriage Sidings and are all that remains of the old seven-road West Yard that extended over the car park. Only the right-hand road remains now as a short siding serving the Network Rail compound. The photograph was taken from Salisbury West signalbox by Pete Warren who was the signalman. The box has also gone.

(*above*) Hampshire unit 1401 emerging from Fisherton Tunnel working a Portsmouth Harbour to Salisbury stopping service on 6 June 1986. (*Dave Baldwin*)

(*below*) 50007 *Sir Edward Elgar* working the 09:40 Exeter St Davids to Waterloo rushing by 47287, which is stood in the old up platform at Dinton station with the MoD Chilmark to Salisbury East Yard freight on 19 May 1988. 47287 will set back out and over the ground frame controlled crossover onto the single line once 50007 has left the single line at Wilton. (*Keith Usher*)

Gary Pollard

Driver at Salisbury

In 1973 I was too young to work on the footplate, so started my railway career on the station at Salisbury. I became a junior railman/messenger boy in the Station Manager's office. This involved making tea, being a general dog's body, and delivering notices and supplies to all the different offices, workplaces and signalboxes at Salisbury. I was given the chance to be placed on a scheme called Job Rotation; this meant that I got to work with different people and jobs around Salisbury station. My first assignment was in the parcels office, which was located on platform 4 (the current Signal box is now situated in the former parcel room). I was taught how to lift heavy items, to load and unload parcels from trains that arrived at the station.

Livestock often arrived at the parcels office. Racing pigeons would arrive in baskets, and we would let them free from the front of the station, then note the time of release and send it back to the owner. There were boxes of young chicks and even hedgehogs for the rescue centre at Tiggywinkles. The most unusual arrival was half a dozen young calves in the brake van area on a passenger train! The mooing of these young animals brought strange looks from the passengers.

My last assignment on Job Rotation was six weeks on the platform as a porter. This is where I got to meet David Shepherd, of artistic fame. David was involved with the West Somerset Railway, a private railway at Cranmore. He would visit Salisbury looking for suitable items for the railway. I helped him to measure the wooden kiosk that stood at the top of the subway ramp between platforms 2 and 3 (a modern version stands in that location today). This was the sort thing he was after. We would make David a cup of tea and he would talk about his locomotive, a BR class 9F called *Black Prince* It was with great delight when, one day, David Shepherd and his loco came through Salisbury on a special. This was the first steam train I had seen since steam had been withdrawn some six or seven years earlier.

To say thank-you to all the staff at Salisbury he presented a signed print of one of his paintings, *Nine Elms, The Last Hours*, and he wrote on it: 'To all my friends at Salisbury, David Shepherd'. This print now hangs on the wall in the Customer Service Office on platforms 2 & 3. The inscription has faded, but can just still be made out.

One of the first steam specials to run through Salisbury was David Shepherd's 92203 *Black Prince*, seen here passing East Yard on 20 August 1975. (*Pete Warren*)

(*above left*) Salisbury driver Barry Symons was the fireman on 48151 when it was to work a test train to Romsey and back on 30 June 1988. Barry was one of our unlucky drivers being responsible for several mishaps including a collision in Salisbury West Carriage Sidings which brought about the withdrawal of 33112 *Templecombe*. (*Keith Usher*)

(*above right*) On 48151 are Eric Cave (on the left) and Roger Smith. Eric was another driver who relished the chance to have a go at driving steam engines again; he has since retired. Roger used to race pigeons and would very often give you a box to take on your journey and ask you to release the bird at your destination; Roger retired early. (*Andy Beavis*)

Salisbury driver Ray Witt on 48151 on 26 June 1988. Sadly Ray has since past away. (*Keith Usher*)

34092 *City of Wells*, waiting in Salisbury East Yard to work a demonstration freight, is passed by 48151 which has just returned from Romsey on a test run on 30 June 1988. (*Paul Abbott*)

Mick Whitcher

Guard at Salisbury

We now move on to one of our most popular guards.

In January 1972 I was lucky enough to have a cab ride from Waterloo to Portsmouth Harbour arranged through my brother-in-law Keith Bacon who was a secondman. I enjoyed the day so much I thought this is the job for me. Next day I went up to the railway station at Salisbury to ask for a job. I saw the then Station Manager, Owen Faisey, who said that unfortunately there were no driver's jobs, but said that he would send me for a medical and if I passed that he would take me on as a guard! I passed the medical and the following week started on the railway. I used to enjoy working on freight trains that had a brake van on as once you got under way it was so peaceful. If you had a smooth-running van and nice warm fire going you could nod off for a while; trouble was, when I awoke, several times I would be looking out the back of the van and think, oh my goodness where has the train gone? Of course, just turn around the other way and there it was.

I remember working an engineer's train from Woking to Eastleigh once; it was a warm summer's evening and we left Woking around 6.00pm. The train had a few empty ballast wagons, two low-mac wagons, one of the last steam cranes in service and then my brake van. The train was unfitted (no brake, only on the class 47 loco and my brake van) and was restricted to 15mph because of the steam crane. As we trundled down the slow line to Basingstoke I had a cup of tea and my sandwiches, every now and then taking a look out and making sure all was well. After Basingstoke I went and stood out on the forward veranda; we were allowed to keep running and I was enjoying the evening sun. As we rounded the curve before Popham tunnels the cab door on the steam crane suddenly swung open on the off-side which meant it would hit anything coming in the opposite direction. I started to wind the hand brake on in my brake van but knew it would not make a lot of difference and hoped the driver would look back and see my frantic waving. As we approached Micheldever, to my horror I saw a passenger train coming, but luck was with me this day as the lines here pull away from each other, the station platform being in the middle of the tracks, and as we slowly went through one side the 12-car fast screamed through on the other. Now, my second bit of luck happened; as we curved round the opposite way the tilt

of the line slammed the crane's door shut! I unwound my handbrake slowly and sighed a huge sigh of relief. Shortly after we recessed in Wallers Ash loop; I made sure all doors on the steam crane were locked!

Mind you, I was not so fortunate a few years later. I was working a van train from Southampton to Clapham Junction and at Eastleigh we had a change of engine and a coach put on that had come fresh and pristine from the works. The engine was 33025, an engine that had a jinx on me. I coupled the engine and coach to the rest of the vans, did a brake test, gave the driver his load sheet, then went and settled into the back cab of 33025. We left Eastleigh on time, next stop Basingstoke. We passed through Winchester going well at 75mph but as we went by Alton Junction a down 91 Weymouth train consisting of 8TC and 4REP passed us and there was an almighty bang with something just missing my side window and smashing into the pristine first coach. My driver had obviously heard it and made an emergency brake application and I thought the down train must have had a door open and that was what had hit us. I went through the engine room to the front cab; in the engine room there was a large hole in the body side. I told the driver about the hole and we decided to put down track circuit clips on the opposite running line (the clips operate the track circuits to put the preceding signal back to danger) and walk back down the line to inspect our train and to see if anyone had fallen out of the down train. The front coach of our train had sustained a fair bit of damage along the side but looked OK to run. We contacted the signalman at the next telephone and told him we had found nothing; he informed us that the down train was at Winchester and that the restaurant car on the REP unit had several windows smashed and body side damage, but there was only one casualty – the buffet steward who was cut by glass. We were instructed to pick up the track circuit clips and take our train on to Basingstoke as quickly as possible where it would terminate. The REP went straight into Eastleigh works, the 8TC units carrying on to Weymouth hauled by a class 33 diesel locomotive. I was informed two days later that it was the engine room side access door that had come open, being sucked open by the passage of the down Weymouth train; the engine had been receiving attention at Eastleigh during the night and the fitter had not locked the door properly (he was suspended for three days as a result). The engine room door had been found in a field after a woman walking her dog had reported nearly being hit by it! The pristine coach returned to Eastleigh works for repairs.

One of the best trains to work was the bullion train from Southampton Docks to Waterloo. The three special CCT vans and BG coach were kept in a secret location within the docks. You would pick the train up at the Millbrook Dock gates, the vans pushed out by one of the dock's 07 shunting engines and a class 74 electro-diesel would be attached to the front. You would then be escorted round the train by dockyard police whilst you carried out the brake test. Two travelling policemen would ride in the BG coach on the rear and were in contact with the driver via the then latest technology, a very large radio! The guard would ride in the back cab of the loco. As soon as you had got the train ready you would leave and once you got the road the dockyard police would sigh with relief and shout: 'You're on your own now, good luck.' Once under way you would always have green signals all the way to Waterloo, the train was not allowed to be stopped. The class 74 locos, or Boosters as they were nicknamed, were quite fast and nippy but also quite bouncy, so you had a lively ride. On arrival at Waterloo a 350 shunting engine would attach at the rear and immediately shunt the vans into one of the dock roads (two short roads in the middle of the platforms at the country end of the station) where the vans were unloaded, surrounded by police!

After 33 years on the railway I retired early. What I miss the most is the camaraderie; everyone worked together and there was always plenty of banter. They were great days!

Mick was a great guard to work with; he always had the banter. My brothers and I called him Dad as he always greeted you with 'All right, my son?'

From 29 October 1951 O.V. Bulleid-designed diesels began a regular diagram of two trips a day from Waterloo to Exeter Central, 687 miles per day. 10202 is seen here at Salisbury in 1952. Weighing 135 tons and powered by an English Electric 16 cylinder 16SVT engine with Napier 75100 turbo charger giving 1,750hp (10203 2,000hp) they were geared to run up to 110mph although in June 1952, 10202 was re-geared to run up to 85mph but accelerate quicker. The locos were fuelled each day at Waterloo; each Sunday they visited Nine Elms for servicing. They were joined in March 1953 by Ivatts 10000 and 10001 and in April 1954 by 10203. In April 1955 all five moved to Camden for West Coast duties, never to return. By the end of 1963 the three Bulleids had been withdrawn. The EE engine went on to be developed into 2,000hp unit for class 40 locos, 2,700hp charging air-cooled unit for class 50 and MkIII 3,250hp unit for class 56. (*Mick Price collection*)

Phil 'Pancho' Gaulton

Driver standrds manager at Salisbury

Now if you have ever been caravanning and seen a man supporting a moustache that looked heavier than he did, then you have seen our next contributor!

I don't know who started the nickname but it stuck right from day one.

I started in March 1970 as an engine cleaner at Salisbury and subsequently passed as a secondman. I then transferred to Woking later that year to get my secondman's position on an '8b' move and came back to Salisbury the following year. I passed for driving in 1978 with 'Colonel' Ted Lynch and became a passed secondman at Salisbury.

In December 1978 I transferred to Westbury on the Western Region to get my driver's job and the rivet holes for the copper plate are still on the back of my neck! The majority of the work at Westbury was freight, with some passenger work between Bristol, and Weymouth/Salisbury, and express passenger work between Paddington and Exeter.

I returned to Salisbury in August 1985 as a driver and became a traction inspector in April 1991, along with Bob Silk. Following a management reshuffle in 1994, I became a train crew supervisor at Salisbury and had my nickname changed to 'Pen Mill Phil'. If Phil was on duty, the route learner always ran and the driver didn't get an early day.

During another management reshuffle in 2000, I became a driver manager at Salisbury where I am now. The one incident that I will own up to is setting the station roof on fire with the flames from the boiler exhaust while steam heating a train in platform 1 at Salisbury. Regarding other incidents, including the run-away train down Savernake Bank on the Berks & Hants line, the buffers falling off a Class 56 loco while shunting in Eling Wharf at Totton, putting a brake van over the top of the stop blocks in the Up Yard at Westbury and almost landing on the up main line, etc., I have always claimed my innocence.

Phil is my immediate manager and he will say he's worked off his feet looking after me. I say I'm pleased he does!

The winners of the 1979 British Rail Staff Association fresh-water fishing competition was the team from Salisbury. From left to right are Dan Matthews, Bob Smith (presenting the cup for BRSA), Dan Matthews Jnr, David Franks and Phil 'Pancho' Gaulton. (*Phil Gaulton collection*)

(*above*) Essential repairs being carried out to bridge 232 over the River Avon at Salisbury. Both up and down main lines were lifted, requiring trains to run via East Yard reception road, seen in the foreground on 28 March 1987. (*Keith Usher*)

(*below*) On the same day 50025 *Invincible* works the 13.10 Waterloo to Exeter St Davids through East Yard reception road during the bridge repairs. Trains were regulated through the section using a pilotman. In this case John 'Lardy' Hill can be seen on the left in the cab, the driver is Salisbury's Tom Gurd. (*Keith Usher*)

Brush Comfort Left Me Battered and Bruised

by Jon Bowen, driver at Salisbury

It had been a long, cold, exhausting winter's night in January 1983; I had been rostered together with driver Bob Thompson for the night as his secondman on an engineer's train which was to drop ballast all evening out at Codford. We had been on the go for the entire shift, running up and down discharging roughly 12 'Sealion' wagonloads of ballast onto the tracks. Eventually we finished and took our class 33 and empty wagons on to Westbury where we put the train into the yard and left it. We then had over an hour to wait for the first passenger train back home to Salisbury, but the yard foreman said to us that a Westbury crew were ready to leave with the Fareham stone train (this had to pass through Salisbury to get to Fareham). We dashed over to their train and they agreed they would slow down for us at Salisbury so we could jump out of the back cab and they would not get a lost time ticket. So Bob and I climbed into the back cab of the Brush, class 47 loco and crashed out in the seats with our feet up in the window. It was lovely and warm with the heaters on full so it wasn't long before we both nodded off to sleep. The next thing I knew was Bob nudging my arm and saying 'Gramshaw' (this is a foot crossing about a quarter of a mile from Salisbury station). I was nearly comatose and struggled to make sense of things. I slowly gained consciousness and then realised I had a problem. As I went to stand up my legs just gave out from under me and I collapsed in a heap back in the seat. I had completely lost all circulation in my legs from having them up in the window for well over an hour. I then managed to stand up again and tried moving them about and stamping them to get some feeling back into them. By now, though, the platform loomed large and Bob had the cab door open ready to jump. I glanced at the speedo, it was reading 15mph, and I thought to myself: 'This is going to hurt'. With that, Bob jumped and made a perfect landing, then the amp meter came to life as the driver started to take power again. I had to jump now or go on to Fareham. So I picked my bag up and went for it. What a mistake – my legs just didn't respond the way they should and I was sent careering down platform 2, legs flailing, arms swinging, bag sent flying. I came to rest as I hit the confectionery machine, much to the amusement of Bob and all the regulars waiting for the 08.12 to Waterloo. My bag split open, the contents scattered all over, breaking my Bardic lamp and tea cup, denting my tea can, sending my tea bags all over the tracks and coffee across the platform. As for me, I had cut both my knees and elbow and because the feeling was now back in my legs they flipping hurt – ouch! But we had got home 23 minutes early!

Driver Jon Bowen is seen cleaning the windscreen on 33112 *Templecombe* prior to working the special on to Waterloo on 14 May 1988. 33026 is the other loco. (*Mike Pearce*)

(*above*) Foster Yeoman were the first firm to operate their own locomotives on British Rail, choosing General Motors to build them, a decision that was not met with much enthusiasm by BR employees (who are still not wild about the locos), but of course led to a lucrative contract for GM. 47294 is seen passing through Salisbury hauling four class 59s from Southampton Docks to Merehead on 24 January 1986. (*Jon Bowen*)

(*below*) 40083 from York depot turned up at Salisbury working a Carlisle Kingmore to Chilmark special MoD freight on 6 July 1983. The engine was supposed to have come off the train at Bescot, then again at Reading but there were no replacements available, so Salisbury driver Mike Wallen (seen standing on platform 3) was sent to Basingstoke to conduct the Saltley crew down to Salisbury where the train was shunted to East Yard and tripped down to Dinton early next day. Another Salisbury driver conducted the crew into the yard and back light engine to Basingstoke. (*Robin Coles*)

John Jackson

Mobile Operations Manager for Network Rail at Salisbury

Let's switch departments again.

When I left school in the early 1970s a career on the railways was the last thing on my mind; in fact, I had no idea whatsoever what I wanted to do. I eventually opted for an apprenticeship as a motor vehicle technician with Edwards Ford in Salisbury. However, after duly completing my training I discovered that this was not the career for me and I soon got fed up of having perpetually black, oily hands and of the cold, concrete-floored workshop environment.

It was quite by chance that one day whilst I was perusing the job opportunities in the local Job Centre (there were plenty of jobs about then) I saw two, one as a postman and the other with British Rail as a signalman. Now, I have to be honest that I wasn't sure what the post of signalman entailed as I had never had any interests in trains or railways but it sounded intriguing. I opted to go for both of them and after various interviews was offered jobs with both the post office and BR. After some thought I decided to take up the position as signalman and this was the starting point of a railway career.

After the usual stint working on the platforms that enabled newcomers to get a feel and understanding of railway workings I was sent out to start my training at Wilton South. Now, this was a completely alien environment to me and it became very clear that I had a lot to learn. After completing my training and 'passing out' for the box I began life as a signaller, a fine breed of gentlemen!

Quickly, it became apparent that there were some great characters working on the railways and I remember one flagman that I always seemed to get at weekends for engineering work. Jock O'Dea (God rest his soul) would always fall up the steps of the signalbox on a Saturday night. One time he went down these steps to go and put his protection down and promptly fell off the platform edge; I don't think that he felt it though! Another time, after putting his detonator protection down on the Up and Down Warminster lines it started snowing with blizzard-like conditions, resulting in the line 'possession' being cancelled. Jock went out to pick up the protection and came back an hour later looking like a yeti, explaining that he couldn't find the detonators.

As in life all good things must come to an end and Wilton South was closed when Salisbury Panel took over. I was transferred to Codford signalbox and also covered Upton Lovell crossing for Mrs Trott to have rest days. Who could forget a cup of Mrs Trott's tea – yuk! My days at Codford were numbered and eventually Codford box also became a casualty of re-signalling.

I was then attached to the minor works Signal & Telegraph gang as their hand signaller. They were installing new AHBs (Automatic Half Barriers) at various locations and I had some great times helping out with pulling cables. We had some good card schools at lunchtimes in the back of the yellow lorries and thinking about it I always seemed to lose money!

Eventually, a signalling post came up as a rest day relief signaller at Gillingham that also covered Templecombe and Tisbury Gates, and I was lucky enough to get the post. So, there we were, me as rest day relief and Garry Shaftoe as general purpose relief – boy, did we have the overtime rostering hours sorted out. We worked some long hours but by then, of course, we had mortgages and families to pay for.

Stan Flood and Ern Day at Templecombe were great characters. 'Floody' would always give me grief because I could never get the old coke boiler to go properly, so it was always cold when he came in to relieve me. There were interesting times when the station reopened and we had to do tickets, parcels, and deal with the public. Sid Dunn at Tisbury Gates was a great bloke, always letting us go early as long as we picked himself and Margaret up from the *South Western Hotel* outside Tisbury Station. He also had the locals well trained as nobody used the crossing after 22.00 hours.

I used to enjoy weekend nights in Gillingham box with Bill Woods as PICOP (Person in Charge of Protection) as I was able to put my feet up in front of the fire and Bill would take over. Sometimes Bill would be elsewhere and I would have Terry Baumber as the flagman. We had some great times. When the possession had been taken we would settle down to our social evening, always keeping an eye on the possession, of course. Starting off with a game of cards we would move on to darts, then a game of draughts. I remember one night he even brought a small snooker table in. The night passed quickly. Happy days – or should that be nights?

(*above*) Tisbury Gates old signal cabin, just west of Tisbury station, viewed on 21 July 1984. The cabin remains but the crossing is now controlled by Automatic Half Barriers. (*Keith Usher*)

(*right*) John Jackson clearing the snow from Templecombe platform in 1984. (*John Jackson*)

Soon after the introduction of Mobile Operations Managers (MOMs) I was lucky enough to be appointed to one of these positions based at Yeovil. Along with 'Blinkin' Bill Waters we were Fast Action Response Teams or FARTS. My assistant for some time was Kevin Goddard, now a signaller at Templecombe. We were called one morning to attend Broom level crossing because of sheep on the line. We pulled up at the crossing and, sure enough, the sheep were on the crossing. What happened next I guess you had to be there to fully appreciate but Kevin turned to me and said: 'You stay here so it doesn't run away and I'll get behind it!' Well, I just collapsed in a heap crying with laughter. Needless to say, that was us finished for the day.

After a few years at Yeovil it was decided by Mr 'Where are you now?' Goodyear that a MOM's post should be created at Salisbury and I was duly appointed.

I have been there ever since and have enjoyed it immensely. I have seen and dealt with so many incidents including derailments, broken rails, faulty points, level crossing incidents, bridge strikes, suicides and many more. That is what makes it such an interesting job; you never know what's going to happen from one day to the next. I guess that I could write a book about my times on the railway; there are so many stories and people that one could talk about. All that I can say is that in my 'nearly 30 years' on the railway it has been an absolute honour and privilege to have known and to have worked with all the guys, many of whom are mentioned in other stories in this book. So, here we are nearly 30 years later, purely by chance and, yes, I might just call it a career after all.

John may not have wanted a career on the railway but he has certainly settled in well and is now one of us.

(*below left*) Wilton South signalbox frame on 22 August 1981. (*John Jackson*)

(*below right*) 33023 runs round its train of ballast at Wilton South on 21 October 1972. It will now go back towards Salisbury wrong road and drop the ballast at the new Wilton Junction that was then in the process of being installed. Passenger services were running from Wilton to and from Exeter, buses being used between Salisbury and Wilton. (*Pete Warren*)

(*above*) On a route-learning trip with Exeter drivers, 121 Bubble car W55018, a Plymouth-based unit, is an unusual visitor at Wilton South in August 1973. (Pete Warren)

(*below*) An un-identified Hymek class 35 approaches Salisbury at Gramshaw crossing on the GWR route. The middle track (the old up road) is now where the stop blocks are situated for the head shunt on the washer road in the Traincare Depot, everything else has gone. The signal was Salisbury 'C' box's longest pull. Note the small children sitting on the crossing. (*Colin Hall*)

The 31s would make a lot of noise and shudder but not much happened; the amps took an age to catch up with all the commotion and then finally they would start to go and, normally with only five coaches on, some nifty running could be achieved. The Spanner steam heat boilers were also a bit hit and miss with some spectacular start-ups if they got flooded. 31419 was a duel-heat example and a regular on the Portsmouth to Cardiff run, seen here passing Salisbury East Yard on 18 April 1979. (*Pete Warren*)

Bob Hardy's Ten-Pennyworth

Driver at Salisbury

Here is Gary Pollard again, tricking the trickster.

Bob Hardy was one of those drivers that were known for 'getting out of work'. One day Bob and I were booked on for the 10.00 cover turn, with me as his secondman for the day. Now Bob would often give his secondman a piece of paper with a phone number on it, and a 10p coin. He would look furtively around the room, even if they on their own, and would say: 'I'm just popping out for a couple of hours; if we get a job ring me on this number'. Hence the 10p. Today was no different and at about 11.30 Bob came over to me with his bit of paper, gave me my instructions and was gone! There I was left to 'hold the fort' and do any shunts – it was easier to do his shunts than to get him to come back.

I used to wonder what he was up to, was it a girlfriend, a good friend, or simply, could it just be his mother? I was always too shy and respectful to ask.

When I saw that Bob would be my driver again on the cover turn the next day I decided to hatch a little plan to get my own back. We booked on as usual, went to the mess room, and made a pot of tea. I sat down, took out the piece of paper that Bob had given me the day before and wrote down the same number on my piece of paper. The drivers in the mess room were talking about their many exploits on the 'steam'. I got up, walked over to Bob, leaned over his shoulder and said 'Bob' and as he looked up, I looked furtively around the room. 'Do you mind if I disappear for an hour; if you need me, I will be on this number', and gave him the bit of paper with the phone number. He nodded and just as I went through the doorway, I caught sight of him looking at the number I gave him. The look on his face as it sunk in that it was same number he had given me the day before was priceless, He got up and shouted: 'You little b**ger'. But too late, I was gone. To this day, I still do not know where Bob used to go.

I think all of us at some time or another was in possession of Bob's ten pence!

Due to engineering work closing the line between Yeovil and Exeter in July 1985 a shuttle service was run from Salisbury and Yeovil. Unusually a Bristol-based DMU was used on Sunday 14 July. (*Andy Clarke*)

Nigel Pearce

Senior Conductor at Salisbury

Nigel Pearce has been on the railway for 24 years, starting as a shunter in Salisbury East Yard. He is now a Senior Conductor, still at Salisbury. Here are two stories from him, the first an account of what he says was 'a lucky day in my career', the second a funny encounter with a passenger.

One day I was working an early Salisbury to Waterloo commuter service formed of a class 50 loco and 9 coaches. We left Basingstoke on time and the 50 got us up to 100mph with ease. As we whizzed through Fleet I was in the second coach from the front walking back to my van after finishing my ticket check when there was a large bang from under the coach, the saloon lights went out, dust filled the carriage and the train came to an abrupt halt filling me with a nervous dread. My commuters on the other hand were still reading their FTs and broadsheets! I looked out of the window but could see nothing amiss, but I could hear air leaking out, so I got down and headed for the engine to see if my driver Ken Blake, one of our most respected senior drivers, could explain.

As I walked along I noticed that the main reservoir and brake pipes were uncoupled between the engine and front coach, I coupled them both back up but could still hear the air leak. I carried on to the front cab and asked Ken: 'Did we hit something?' 'No, nipper', was the reply. I told him about the pipes and the air leak.

'The leak is what has stopped us, we have lost main reservoir air pressure', said Ken. I went back to the pipes between the engine and coach and shut the cocks on the main reservoir pipes, went back to the cab and asked Ken: 'Has that done the trick?' 'Yea, well done nipper, give me a brake test when you get back in your van and if its OK, we'll go'. This I did and we carried on working brake pipe only, a practice most air brake pipe trains run by now.

We had asked for a Carriage and Wagon fitter to check the train at Woking but none was available and we were told to carry on to Waterloo. We arrived safely at Waterloo and a fitter met us and had a look around. Ken and I could not work out what had gone wrong; the fitter came to us and asked: 'What the hell did you hit?'. 'Nothing', said Ken. 'You have, as there's a huge gorge running down the middle of the under frame and gear on the front two coaches and a large gash in the main res pipe on the front coach, that's where you lost all your air'. We were all now puzzled. The fitter carried on looking around and then gave us a shout: 'Come 'ere, round the front, notice anything missing?'. 'No, can't say I do', said Ken. 'Look', said the fitter 'no screw coupling! That's what you hit'. We were booked to go down to Clapham empties with the train; the 50 was booked to remain on the rear and another loco went on the front and took us to Clapham. When at Clapham we took the opportunity to have a look at the

Salisbury guard Nigel Pearce was glad the train arrived early as he had time to go down the slide! (*Gary Pollard*)

damage; what a mess under the first two coaches. We were lucky that the coupling flew out and missed the wheels; at 100mph there could have been a problem. Next day we were informed the coupling had been found in the 'ten foot' (the large gap between the up and down lines), two miles short of Farnborough. The 50 and two coaches had gone to Old Oak Common for assessment; all agreed we had had a lucky day!

I was working the 19.53 Salisbury to Exeter St Davids one evening and we were waiting for departure time when a gentleman came staggering up to me with a huge grin on his face and a loaf of sliced bread in his hands. He said to me: 'I'sh goings to Gillingham, hic, please, hic, pleashe can you wake me's up when we, when we'sh, hic, get there?' I smiled back and said: 'yea, no worry, sit just inside by the door mate and get yer head down'. Once we were under way I went to check tickets and came straight across the gentleman with the loaf of bread. He said 'I am in soo much trouble, I set out from home in Gillingham this morning at just after nine, the wife sent me out to get a loaf of bread, ah this very loaf here in facts. When I

came outs the bakers I bumped into an old friend of mine who I hadn't seen for years and he said he was going up to Salisbury to meet some other old mates and asked me to come along, so me and the loaf of bread have had a very enjoyable day, buts we are both probably gonna be toast when we's gets in, please don't let me oversleep Gillingham or I be in the s***'. Well all the other passengers and myself are all laughing and I promise to make sure he and the loaf at least get off the train. We arrive at Gillingham, a fellow passenger has already woken the gentleman, and he staggers off the train thanking everyone and saying: 'Wish me luck, I gonna need it', but I notice he hasn't got the loaf of bread so I quickly looked at where he had been sitting and there it was, squashed flat as he had fallen asleep on it. I took it out to him and handed it back to him. He looked at me despondently and said: 'Oh f***, I'm dead'. I turned, shut the doors on the train and we left. He was still stood motionless staring at the squashed loaf as we departed. I have never seen the gentleman since but always have a slight chuckle when buying a loaf of sliced bread!

20158/175 working The Severn Choppers railtour into Salisbury in 1983. (*Colin Hall*)

(*above*) Driver Lionel Blake (left) with his fireman for the day, driver Brian Hawes, on A4 4498 *Sir Nigel Gresley* waiting for the road at Salisbury with the 10:07 to Yeovil Junction on 25 October 1986. (*Keith Usher*)

(*above right and below*) Charlie Stone (left) and Doug Harding about to have fun with A4 4498 *Sir Nigel Gresley* on 10 July 1988 on its journey fron Salisbury to Yeovil. Charlie was a driver who loved his job, and the opportunity to work on steam again thrilled him; unfortunately he passed away soon after his retirement. Doug enjoyed a flutter on the horses and a good holiday. He retired early, he assures us not off his winnings! (*above right, Andy Beavis; below, Paul Abbott*)

Kevin Regan

Driver at Salisbury

Kevin started as a Trainman D, went on to become a driver, and later moved to the Training Centre at Basingstoke before he returned to Salisbury to resume driving duties. Here 'The Guv' tells a tale or two.

Trainman's Tales

Nights paid better in those days and at Salisbury we were often sent on loan to Eastleigh which had a lot of work going on at that time with the electrification of the Botley and Netley roads. On one such occasion I went over on a set of empties from Salisbury to Eastleigh, reported to the Train Crew Supervisor and were told that there were 12 hours available for the taking. So it was with an Eastleigh driver that I was taken in one of the yellow staff vans to the bottom of an embankment somewhere on the Botley road. We got to the loco and saw the crew we were relieving who said that they had hardly moved in the previous 10 hours so we could expect a quiet night. The train was a load of copper wire on large drums and we were informed by the Permanent Way crew that they had to go off somewhere else in the possession so we could

Kevin 'The Guv' Regan working his first train, 159005, after passing for driving in 1997. (*Kevin Regan collection*)

get our heads down for a while. Well, this while turned out to be over nine hours. When the Permanent Way team got back they found both the driver and me asleep in the loco and most of the copper wire stolen! There then followed a frank and meaningful exchange that resulted in the Eastleigh driver and I having to report to our respective bosses the following day. As it turned out this was an inside job with some of the Permanent Way gang working with local gypsies.

Towards the end of loco-hauled trains, reliability reached an all-time low and it was not unusual to break down two or more occasions in one shift. This got the punters' backs up and some of them started a book to bet on how far they would get each day or if they would get there at all. For a short time all the trains terminated at Basingstoke despite the fact that there were no planned or emergency engineering works on. One of the more interesting failed trains was at Feniton, where in those days the loco would pull onto the road crossing so that the first coach would be positioned perfectly on the platform. I gave the Ready To Start light, we moved a few feet, and all went silent. I got onto the loco and spoke to the driver who then walked around it but could find nothing wrong until he checked the fuel gauge only to see that we were out of fuel! By this time there was a quite a queue of traffic building up on both sides of the crossing and the crossing keeper told the drivers to find alternative routes as we would be there for some time. I went and informed the passengers who were not best pleased but after telling them that there was a pub opposite the station the mood improved. Most then left the train and headed for the pub. Two hours later a Class 37 from Exeter arrived to pull the train to Exeter and I went into the pub to tell the punters that we were, at last, ready to go. The landlord had to ring the last orders bell to get their attention but he was pleased with the increase in his takings, as it had been a quiet night until the train arrived.

In 1992 a number of steam specials were run from Salisbury to Yeovil and Exeter and it was the first time that steam had gone as far as Exeter for over 25 years. The loco was a recently overhauled Merchant Navy class with Don Macey as driver and Richard Cottrell as fireman for the first part and the Traction Inspector was Roy Porter. The load was 13 coaches, heavy by the standards of the time, and it was a baking hot day.

The train was booked to pass an up train at Gillingham then fast to Yeovil Junction where we were booked for 20 minutes before going on to Exeter. After leaving Gillingham and passing through Buckhorn Weston Tunnel we really started to move! The stopwatch brigade on board was keeping a close eye on the speed, which officially was 75mph. Even to me, it was obvious that we were going a fair bit faster than that. Down through Sherborne we hit 96mph and I understand that Roy Porter put his hand on Don Macey's shoulder and said: 'Slow down now, you've had your fun!' Needless to say, we arrived at Yeovil Junction early. I went to the loco to get on the footplate and what hit me was the massive heat. Rich was sat at the back near the tender and Roy passed me a shovel and told me to climb onto the tender to shovel down the coal to him while he shovelled it into the firebox – we had used a lot of coal on Don's run.

Driving tales on 159s are much more boring but one incident will make you smile. I was working an Exeter to Paignton train on a rain-soaked, windy day in March. I had a route learner with me who was doing the driving. We got stopped along the sea wall between Dawlish Warren and Dawlish with a signal at red. The only way to contact the signaller is by the Signal Post Telephone so without so much as a coat I got off the unit to use the SPT and just as I did so a wave broke over the wall, soaking me completely and knocking me onto the ballast just as the signal changed to proceed! I remember that I drove the rest of the journey so that I could attempt to dry off next to the cab heater.

155313 arrives at Salisbury with a Portsmouth to Cardiff service on 24 July 1989. These were the first Sprinter units that Salisbury drivers were trained on in 1991. (*Robin Coles*)

156 units were employed on the Portsmouth to Cardiff trains for a short while until 158 units became available. 156472 arrives at Salisbury on 11 February 1989. This unit is now allocated to Newton Heath depot in Manchester. (*Robin Coles*)

Some of the best jobs we used to get were working special trains. These two photos show Salisbury crews on tour.

(*right*) In 1978 a special was run by the Lea Valley Railway Club to Meldon and Meeth with loco 33109. The crew posing at Meeth are, from left to right, Jack Tandy (guard; his son Robin is still a driver at Salisbury), Adrian Stewart (secondman, now a driver at Salisbury), Ron 'Tigger' Pearce (driver, now retired) and Bob Dat (Exeter pilot driver. Bob was a character; whenever he came up to Salisbury he would tell us his stories of flying Lancaster bombers in the war). The tour went well even though a flock of sheep got on the line at Okehampton; there was enough crew to round them up! (*Adrian Stewart collection*)

(*below*) Salisbury crew of driver Ted Hooper and secondman Roger Long worked the 'Gunnislake Goliath' railtour on 21 December 1985 and they are seen here at Cattlewater, Plymouth. The tour lasted all day and involved two Salisbury crews, the other pair being driver Brian Hawes and secondman Jon Bowen. (*Roger Long collection*)

Gemma Hirst

Commercial guard at Salisbury

Back to our stories now and one from Gemma that shows the value of schools' work experience schemes.

I joined the railway in September 2000 aged 16 as a Signal & Telecommunications trainee technician, working for Balfour Beatty at the Salisbury depot in Churchfields Road. I decided to join the railway after doing two weeks' work experience with South West Trains whilst still at school. Everyone made me feel I was part of a family, helping out with jobs, acting as a team and getting things done. I decided that this was definitely the career for me as that's the kind of person I am.

On my first day on the railway the other trainees and myself all had to meet at Woking to do our personal track safety (PTS) course which gave us the basic knowledge to walk on or near the running lines. It was quite daunting as I was the only girl on the course and on many courses thereafter. On completion of the course I and one other trainee returned to Salisbury where we met the teams that I worked with for the next three years. This is where the work and fun began.

All of my colleagues had different characters with some still set in their ways, as many old railway men are. Nevertheless, they still treated me like one of the family and as 'one of the lads', as once again, I was the only girl to be working with Salisbury S&T, out of a team of 19 men. The men would put up their womanly calendars and I would put up posters of men; no one minded, it was just a bit of mess room banter. I used to particularly like working in the Wylye area during the summer months when I would make my team mates walk ahead of me, only to watch them suddenly jump up in the air when they spotted adders basking in the sun. The winter months were bitterly cold in that area as the wind and rain would beat off the hills.

On one particular early shift, just as we were due off duty, a fault came in for the Whitchurch area. Off we went from Porton in the van discussing what the problem might be. On arrival at the site, as we started to park the van it slipped in mud and got wedged up against the railway fence; the wing mirror came round and hit the window, making the men jump from their seats. I clambered out from the rear seats to the front. Off we went to fix the problem on the track and after it was rectified we returned to the van only to wonder how we could get out and back home.

We phoned the RAC who had no hope of getting us out but another S&T team turned up to help us push the van with me trying to drive it, even though I couldn't drive at the time. We were well and truly stuck and to make matters worse the van was running out of diesel, dusk was falling and everyone was getting hungry. Our only option was to wait for our supervisor with a winch to get us out. In the meantime we stood around with our arc lights on, telling jokes to one another to keep spirits up. Needless to say it was a very long day as we got home around 21.30 that night after starting at 06.30.

Working night turns could also be quite fun. Another team member and I would send a man around to the next railway access point in the van whilst we walked the line doing our maintenance in between. We would then lie in wait for our mate to join us and as he approached jump out on him from the bushes. You can imagine the reaction of the 'victim'...

I did many courses and loved being out and about with the lads having a laugh, braving the wet and cold, walking the lines in all winds and weathers and also learning from my work mates, fixing equipment and maintaining equipment along the way. An office job definitely isn't for me; there was nothing better than getting my hands oily in a dirty set of trackwork points.

Working for the S&T was a fun and challenging time but after three years I decided it was time to move on. This is when I joined my father at South West Trains where we both work as commercial guards at Salisbury. I have currently been in this role for 4½ years and it's very enjoyable in a completely different way to working as part of the S&T team. I get to meet so many passengers with a wide range of characters and personalities and work with a great team of such individuals.

Gemma has certainly settled in well and is well respected by her peers. It wouldn't surprise me if Gemma has a go at driving one day; I'm sure she would do well at that also.

(*above*) A strong gang waiting for the arrival of 159002 which had made a special trip to Waterloo driven by Mike Dawkins in June 1993; from left to right are Nigel Brodwick (Station Manager) Garry Shaftoe (Train Crew Supervisor) Bob Silk (Driver Standards Manager), unknown, and Steve Horne (driver). (*Steve Anderson*)

(*below*) 159002 has arrived back after her special run to Waterloo. This is the unit that went on to be named *City of Salisbury* and has now covered over three million miles. (*Steve Anderson*)

Andy Haddon

Safety Standards & Emergency Planning Manager for South West Trains

Next Andy Haddon reflects; his commuting 'mileometer' must have gone round the clock.

My first real memories of Salisbury and the West of England line date back to the very early seventies during my last years at school. I used to go train-spotting at Eastleigh from my home in Bognor Regis and on one such trip decided to make the additional ride on to Salisbury – to be quite honest I cannot remember much about it apart from my first classic view of Salisbury Cathedral as the train swept down into the station from the tunnel. Round about that same time I also did a trip from Bognor, travelling up to Waterloo via Clapham Junction then catching a Crompton (Class 33)-hauled train of Western Region Mark 1 coaches down to Exeter St Davids, returning on the Saturdays only through service to Brighton, which at that time was operated with Hastings Line narrow-bodied Diesel Electric Multiple Units.

There was something instantly appealing in arriving at Salisbury – to me it was, and still is, the gateway to the West Country. It was not until 18 years later when we bought our house in Templecombe during 1989 that I reacquainted myself with Salisbury and the line down to Yeovil and Exeter. It was from this point onwards that I really got to know the route; its staff and passengers.

I have now been commuting on the West of England line for nearly 20 years and have seen much change in that time, including rail privatisation, the demise of the Class 50s, 47s, 33s and Hampshire units, the introduction of the Class 159 fleet and the current robust timetable for the route.

I must admit, I was not really sorry to see the last of locomotive-hauled trains – there is nothing worse on a very cold January morning than riding on a train hauled by a diesel without train heating ability, or finding out that the replacement locomotive for your train's failed one was still 45 or more minutes away!

The introduction of the Class 159 fleet was initially met with trepidation by our passengers (myself included!) but over the years they have proved their worth by providing a reliable and efficient train service that our customers really do appreciate – honestly, remember I travel with them practically every weekday!

Having met, worked with and assisted staff who work at Salisbury and on the West of England line in general, I can also say that I have not met a more friendly and conscientious group of railway personnel which has made my commuting a much more enjoyable experience than it might have been!

Salisbury driver Mike Dawkins gets ready to leave the reception road with the 10:49 Salisbury to Dinton MoD on 1 February 1989. His guard Dick Hunt can just been seen on the secondman's side of 47289. (*Keith Usher*)

08831 moves 03079 in Salisbury East Yard on 21 October 1983. The 03 was en-route from Gateshead to Eastleigh works for modifications to allow it to work on the Isle of Wight. (*Colin Hall*)

(*below*) 08831 shunts in Salisbury East Yard for the last time on 1 May 1987. From the following week Salisbury would not have an 08 on pilot duties and driver Jock Bell who was the resident shunt driver was displaced. The 08 was kept 'under the wall' in Fisherton Yard from around 16.00 till 08.00. It was used to shunt the parcel vans in the late afternoon and then take the vans off the paper train at 03.30. Jock would sign on at 08.00 and take the 08 up to East Yard, do a day's shunting and bring it back by 16.00. Jock would not be happy if the loco was used and the fuel header tank was not pumped to maximum, or the hand brake screwed on too hard, the door left open, the cab left dirty, and heaven forbid if you forgot to knock out the battery-isolating switch as this would lead to possible flat batteries and throw Jock's daily routine right out of the window! Jock now lives in one of the new houses that were built on the site of East Yard. (*Robin Coles*)

(*above*) During re-signalling of the GWR route to Exeter in 1983 Sunday services were diverted via Salisbury and Westbury. Here 43032 makes a smokey departure with a train for Paddington on 1 May whilst 43177 waits with a Newcastle departure. (*Robin Coles*)

(*below*) A picture taken from Salisbury East signalbox with, unusually, a 9-car DMU formation leaving for Portsmouth. To the right can be seen the British Rail Staff Association clubhouse that was built on the site of the old milk dock after moving from Cherry Orchard Lane where it was situated opposite the old steam shed. The track layout has changed considerably and the club has twice been extended, so that it now borders the track where the front of the DMU is. (*Pete Warren*)

Adrian Stewart

Driver at Salisbury

Andy Haddon has built up an excellent knowledge of the route and always makes himself available to help crews on those rare occasions things go wrong, but even he will admit his knowledge is minuscule compared to our next contributor! Adrian Stewart started on the railways in 1974 and progressed up through the grades to become a driver in 1988. He also trained as a traction trainer and taught many of our present-day drivers all about 159 units, and the railways. He transferred to Merlin Rail and was lucky enough to work again on class 31s, 33s, 37s, 45s, 47s, 50s, 52s and several steam engines. Unfortunately the private rail business is tough and he was made redundant but you can't keep a good man down and he was re-employed by South West Trains and is back again driving at Salisbury. Here are some of his recollections.

My first duty as a secondman was with driver John 'Dolly' Dawkins on 33104 with the breakdown crane, which we took to where the return empty Tiverton to Fawley tanks had become derailed, not a confidence booster for a new recruit.

One Saturday Ren Judd and myself were booked on a Permanent Way works train helping to lay new sleepers on the up road near Codford. Norman Hibbard was working the steam crane, off-loading the sleepers from our train. During the night we pulled up towards Codford. There were some overhead high-voltage cables crossing the railway just there; yes, you've guessed right, Norman hit the wires with the crane, burning a bit out of the jib. I think we made 12 hours that night; Ren was always after a bit more! Unfortunately the surrounding area was without power for nearly three days.

George Tams was one of our older guards who was very laid back and called everyone 'our kid' – I remember being at work one morning; about 04.00 George came in to the mess room to ask if we could help him out as he needed to do some work on his Morris Minor car which was opposite platform 1 in the staff car park. About five of us went down to carry out his request. It turned out that George wanted to turn the car over on its roof. I remember he placed two or three blankets on the ground and then we all lifted his car over onto its roof. We returned to the mess room and about an hour or so later George came back in and asked us to help him turn the car back the right way up. It transpires that George had repaired the brakes! Yet another character gone but not forgotten. Well done, our kid.

One day I was taking 56034 to Exeter on the front of 47715 which was low on coolant. I remember the Exeter driver going for gold as we were 45 minutes late from Salisbury and two minutes early at Honiton! The 56 was to go back to Salisbury on the front of the Meldon stone, but the loco was needed post haste at Woking to work some empties back to Westbury so I brought it back light engine to Salisbury, Keith Usher working on to Woking in what I believe was a record time. It was only when I got back did we realise that class 56 locos were not permitted to travel west of Yeovil!

Adrian has been a fount of knowledge and has helped me with gathering information for this book; he was my instructor for 159 units when I was training to become a traction trainer and his excellent tuition has served me well; oh, and if you need any logs he's your man!

Adrian Stewart on 71000 *Duke of Gloucester* when he was working with Fragonset. (*Adrian Stewart collection*)

118

(*above*) 34092 *City of Wells* is seen approaching Teffont Mill crossing, between Dinton and Tisbury. (*Keith Usher*)

(*below*) *City of Wells* works a demonstration freight from Salisbury East Yard to Fisherton Yard on 30 June 1988. (*Paul Abbott*)

On 14 July 2003, 37308 was in charge of 6Y26, the 08.31 Eastleigh to Quidhampton service, and is seen about to set back into the English China Clay sidings. The ECC facility at Quidhampton closed on 30 March 2009. (*Chris Pelling*)

45143 *5th Royal Inniskilling Dragoon Guards 1685-1985* working the 13:10 Waterloo to Exeter St Davids, arriving at Salisbury on 11 June 1985. There had been a rededication ceremony at Waterloo; Salisbury driver Dave Acton had piloted an Exeter driver and had a drive on the way back! (*Colin Hall*)

The *Life on Mars* cast during a break in filming? Well, not quite. From left to right, Keith Usher (now Operations Manager for South West Trains), Bob Thompson (now a driver at Salisbury) and Andy Beavis (also now a driver at Salisbury). They were all, at the time, secondmen at Salisbury during a lull in their hectic day in 1980. It must have been a chilly day or they are rummaging for something in their pockets! (*Keith Usher collection*)

Tony 'Kovo' Kowalaski (on the left) and driver Henry Ford about to work a demonstration freight through Salisbury to Fisherton Yard with 34092 *City of Wells*. Kovo is still driving at Salisbury and organises many social activities. Henry has passed away but will always be remembered for his coffee that managed to give you a nice warm glow inside! (*Keith Usher*)

Roger Long

Driver standards manager at Salisbury

Next up Roger Long. Along with Brian Anderson they are the pin-up boys of the depot!

I left school in May 1978 and had an interview with Frank Heritage (the then depot manager at Salisbury) and his assistant Martin Chant; not too difficult an interview – I had to write my name and read a passage from a book! I was accepted and started on the railway at Salisbury on 15 June 1978 with a young looking Andy Beavis; we got our first rollicking that day when Andy asked the Train Crew Supervisor Gordon Hooper if we could go home for lunch and were promptly told: 'You're at work now sonny, not at school'. We both went to the Training School at Southampton that first week. I passed the training course and became a traction trainee; I progressed to secondman in 1979 and was sent on my driver's course in November 1982 and six months later, and only just 21, I was passed for driving. As we had 12 passed men at Salisbury and I was the most junior I did not get out driving that much straight away.

By 1987 I was appointed a full-time driver. A year later I started doing the Train Crew Supervisor's job when they were short. I enjoyed it and this started me on a new path in my railway career. In 1991 I became full-time TCS at Basingstoke and six months later became TCS at Salisbury. In 2000 I was Acting Performance Manager at Southampton, before returning again to Salisbury as acting driver standards manager, a job I took full-time in 2002 and I am still doing now.

Here are a few stories I can remember. Driver Bob Hardy and myself once worked a car train to Yeovil Junction for unloading and during the shunt move at Yeovil we had to propel the train onto the car unloading ramp. Stormy Gale was the shunter and kept calling us back. Bob had to apply more power during the move as the train was slowing down; it turned out we had hit the blocks and several wagons had derailed and piled up, writing off a number of brand new cars!

Driver standards manager Roger Long busy keeping the railways running smoothly. In the background (facing) is his colleague Phil 'Pancho' Gaulton telling Steve Fay, sat opposite, of the joys of caravanning. (*Mike Pearce*)

When I was TCS on nights, Martin Iles and myself, one morning after the last London train was in and shunted, made a ball out of sellotape and paper. We used to play football and cricket on platform 4 by the signalbox with Matthew Quinn. That night Martin broke the window in the Railtrack office. We blamed vandals during the night!

We also used to race the tractor used for pulling 'brutes' around. It was a time trial to see who did the fastest circuit. We would start off in the booking hall, turn right, then drive up to the end of platform 6, turn around, then back along platform 6 all the way down platform 4, turn around, then back to the booking hall. We also raced each other with the tractor and the sweeper; one night Martin Iles was racing the sweeper and while going down the subway the brakes failed and he crashed into the wall.

On quiet Sunday afternoons we used to ring the announcer and ask for an announcement to be made for a Hugh Jass to make himself known to any platform staff!

I was down in the subway store at about 03.00 one Sunday morning, putting archives away; a button fell to the floor, I picked it up and it looked like one off of my suit, so I put it in my pocket. Moments later another button fell to the floor the same as before, so I picked it up and looked at my jacket but no buttons were missing. I put this one, too, in my pocket then started to

get a bit paranoid, wondering where the buttons were coming from. Then another button fell to the floor. This time I didn't wait and promptly left the store. Hence the nickname 'buttons' stuck for a few years after. I never did find out where the buttons came from.

Roger has also had the nicknames 'Buxted', 'Shiny' and 'Jim' over the years.

(*right*) In September 1985 the 150th anniversary celebrations of the GWR were held, and BR put on bit of a show in Salisbury platform 6 with a strange mix of locos on display, 47158 *Henry Ford*, 37241 and 33025 *Sultan*. Left in charge for the day were, from left to right, traction inspector Roy Porter (now retired), driver Ken 'Professor' Blake (Ken loved nothing more than to be able to complete the *Telegraph* crossword whilst watching live cricket; he has since passed away) and secondman Roger Long (now driver standards manager at Salisbury and still unable to give any believable excuse as to why he was on his knees). (*Steve Anderson*)

(*below*) 47158 *Henry Ford*, 37241, 33025 *Sultan* and an unidentified SR 3H unit! (*Steve Anderson*)

British Rail — SOUTHERN

B.R. 2072/72

*DRIVER'S/†GUARD'S REPORT

Station/Depot _____ SALISBURY _____

Date ____ 6 May _____ 19 89

Date of Incident ___ Tuesday 18 April ___ 19 89

Place of Incident ____ Woking ____

Delay ____ 45 ____ mins.

Train Reporting No. | I | V | 2 | O | 2038 hrs.

From ___ Waterloo ___

To ___ Yeovil ___

Type of Traction ___ 50 ___

Loco/Unit No. ___ 50018 ___

Load of Train ___ 320 ___ tons

No. of Vehicles ___ 10 ___

No. fitted ___ – ___

Brake force ___ – ___

	Name	Home Station
*Guard xx Shunter xxchange	P Pearce	Salisbury
Driver	A J Beavis	Salisbury
Second Man	–	–

Assisting Loco (if any) No. _____ Driver _____

Type of brake in use ___ Air ___

Whether train loco E.Q. fitted | | YES | / | NO

Position of passenger/goods switch ___ Passenger ___

* Delete as applicable

†GUARDS: Defects in COACHING STOCK to be reported on form B.R. 29206

REPORT (including weather conditions)
GIVE FULL PARTICULARS OF ANY DAMAGE TO TRAINS OR WORKS

I was working the 50018 down with the 2038 Waterloo to Yeovil Junction when running through Weybridge under full power I had complete loss of amps. Traction overload light bright and earth light bright, so I reset overload and coasted to Woking.

On leaving Woking I tried for power but the engine kept overloading, within 2 minutes of leaving time I requested to the Station Supervisor that I required another loco.

20 minutes later the Station Supervisor informed me that it was arranged for 33008 to be put on the front of 50018 for me to haul. 5 minutes later the loco arrived.

I left Woking at 2140 and arrived at Salisbury 2250.

(continue overleaf if necessary)

Signature _____

A driver's report form. These need to be submitted whenever anything goes wrong, which of course is not very often! (*Andy Beavis*)

(*above*) Waiting for the road is 56001 on 09:54 Ardingley to Westbury stone empties on 2 November 1985. The 56s were a powerful engine and would have been well suited to passenger train working, if they were fitted with train heat, as they had surprisingly good acceleration, I managed to out-run a 50 leaving Woking one evening with return stone empties weighing in at 315 tons, compared to the 291 tons for the nine coaches the 50 was pulling. (*Keith Usher*)

(*below*) On the final day of class 50 operation, due to the failure of 50033 *Glorious*, control in their wisdom put 60033 *Anthony Ashley Cooper* on 1V09 08.55 Waterloo to Paignton as far as Salisbury. It was crewed by an Eastleigh driver. (*Nigel Crow*)

David Tattam

Commercial guard at Salisbury

Next to Dave Tattam, someone who can keep a secret.

I have worked on the trains since 2000, starting as a cleaner at Salisbury Traincare Depot for a year before transferring to become a commercial guard in 2001.

Being a guard I have experienced and witnessed many events on the trains along with the emotions and feelings that connect passengers with our daily work.

As a commercial guard my priority is always the safety of everyone connected with the train. Many months of training are given to all guards before being allowed to work a train with the authorisation of a guard's licence. I have, like most guards, experienced people from all walks of life as passengers on the trains and here is a brief outline of just some of those experiences. The young and old, rich and famous, everyone at some point has travelled on a train. Many travel to get to work, for others it may be a shopping trip to London, the beginning of a holiday, or even the start to a honeymoon. No journey is ever the same, which makes the job even more exciting.

I once met a soldier who was off to London to be presented with the George Cross. His deserved excitement was shared with me where he explained his feelings at receiving such a prestigious and recognised medal.

Politicians, comedians, Olympic medallists, celebrity chefs have all travelled on my trains over the years where their purpose is to travel from A to B as quickly and safely as possible. Like myself they are unaware of who will be on their train. Who will they be sat next to? Will the train be on time? Will I get a coffee? Will I get a seat?

Sick and vulnerable people are some of our passengers, who have been fighters and shown great courage and dignity when tackling their personal problems. These inspirational individuals are quite often very reserved about their own issues and it is always a pleasure to assist them in whatever way I can when travelling on my train.

Many things have been left on my trains by passengers including mobile telephones, Christmas presents, glasses, briefcases – you name it, it's been left on a train at some point! But, how could someone forget a bike? Very easy, it's only when the train is pulling out of the station that the passenger realises they're missing something and that the bike that they should be doing 10mph on is continuing down the line at 90mph. Are they then too embarrassed to admit: 'I've left something on the train'?

Exeter, Plymouth, Paignton, London, Southampton, Bristol, Basingstoke, Bath Spa, Keynsham, Gillingham, Yeovil Junction, Chandler's Ford, Romsey and Totton are just a few of the stations that are or have been served directly from Salisbury. On these journeys I have met some wonderful people over the years, both as passengers and as work colleagues, whilst doing a job that I really enjoy. My final part describes a journey that I experienced not long after becoming a guard.

I was working a busy commuter train early one morning. We had just left Andover station and a woman went and sat in the First Class section of one of the coaches. She was wearing casual clothes along with a scraggy looking long cardigan/coat. She stood out against the rest of the passengers in First Class who were all obviously on their way to work at their offices and banks in central London. The newspapers were rustling, the eyebrows being raised. Who was she and did she have any right to be in First Class? I could only imagine the thoughts racing through the minds of the curious passengers and their concerns as to the presence of this person in their section of the train. I approached the lady who informed me that she needed to purchase a ticket to London. After quoting the price of a First Class single ticket a credit card was produced for payment for the fare. Her fellow passengers' concerns had now been answered. She WAS one of them and they were able to return to their papers and work without agitation that someone was sitting in their area without a valid ticket. I carried out the ticket transaction and read the name on the credit card... I now realised who the lady was. She was married to one of the world's greatest rock stars and I was probably the only one on that train, other than herself, that was aware of this. I presented the ticket and credit card to the lady who gave me a wonderful smile and thanked me. She obviously realised that I now knew exactly who she was and that she had allowed me to be part of the secret of her presence on the train.

No, I have no idea who she was; Dave has never said!

An unusual working seen here with 1025 *Western Guardsman* in the English China Clay sidings at Quidhampton. There must have been a Westbury crew on here, as Salisbury men never learnt the Westerns. 1025 was new on 1 November 1963 and withdrawn on 6 October 1975 after clocking up 1,192,000 miles. (*Pete Warren*)

English China Clay at Quidhampton just west of Salisbury have their chalk pit and factory which is rail connected. On 12 June 1985 they were to take delivery of their own shunting locomotive, a Bagnall 0-4-0 diesel hydraulic, works number 8367. Unfortunately the low-loader lorry bringing the engine could not negotiate the hump-backed bridge into the factory entrance so they unloaded the loco at Salisbury East Yard about two miles away. The little loco was not passed to run on the main line, but Albert Cooke the running foreman that day gave Keith Usher the job of piloting the ECC driver from East Yard to Quidhampton 'off the record and as quick as possible'. This Keith duly did but the little loco could not cope with the journey and overheated at Skew Bridge, half a mile from its destination. After waiting 20 minutes the engine had cooled down enough and completed the journey. The cover-up operation that followed was a great success! The upper picture shows the ECC loco preparing to leave as 56001 passes with the 09.54 Ardingley to Westbury stone empties. The lower one shows it waiting to enter Quidhampton sidings after its epic and traumatic journey. (*both photos Keith Usher*)

The final run of the 'Quidhampton tanks' from the English China Clay site took place on Monday 30 March 2009. Service 6Y27 1012 Quidhampton to Eastleigh was hauled by 66193 carrying a suitable name and headboard – 'Quidhampton 1972-2009 The End' – and was signalled by none other than the longest-serving Salisbury signaller John Say. (*Matt Hurst*)

Just Not Cricket!

Another snippet now from Gary Pollard.

At Salisbury in the late 1970s and early 1980s there were quite a few occasions when several secondmen would be hanging around spare at the same time. Ken Blake was a driver whom we used to call 'Professor' because he would often use big words and completed the *Telegraph* crossword on a daily basis. Ken also followed cricket and was always listening to it on the radio. It did not matter what any one else wanted, cricket came first.

On this day, there were about four secondmen sat spare, and we were all listening to Radio 1 through the gramophone in the corner of the mess room. Ken Blake came in, gave us a disapproving look, and retuned the radio to the live cricket match being broadcast at the time. This was typical behaviour for Ken. The next day we (spare secondmen) were listening to Radio 1 again when Ken Blake came in, gave us the same look as the day before, walked over to the gramophone and adjusted the tuning knob. No matter how much he fiddled with it, however, Radio 1 kept blasting out! Ken looked at us,

we were all sitting straight-faced. trying not to smile and with a smug look. Ken turned the radio off but Radio 1 kept on playing. Ken was, by now, getting cross so he leaned over the back of the gramophone and removed the plug from the socket. And, yes, Radio 1 kept on playing and we were giggling like naughty school children. Ken stormed out of the mess room and went to listen to the cricket on his portable radio in private. What Ken had not known was that earlier in the day we removed the back of the gramophone, placed another radio inside with Radio 1 playing, and then replaced the back. The gramophone was then turned on with the tuner volume turned right down so that the display was illuminated and it all looked quite normal. This meant that no matter what Ken did he could not retune the radio!

Ken was a top link driver and expected the respect that went with his position, but he was a true gentleman with a very clever wit. Mind you, he used to take the pressure off the rest of us because if an engine was going to fail it would fail whilst Ken was on it!

RAF Dinton and Chilmark

A two-foot gauge loco named *Trumpton*, used as a fire train at RAF Dinton, photographed on 15 October 1987. (*Keith Usher*)

(*right*) Barclay 0-4-0 loco seen at Teffont Mill crossing, working on the MoD line from Dinton to the RAF depot at Chilmark on what was the old up road, on 20 July 1978. BR locos were banned from using this section although I did work along it twice with 09001 when the Signal & Telegraph Department renewed cabling along the route. Adrian Stewart worked 33025 along the line to pick up a special train, at the gates to the complex, carrying bombs destined for Harrier jump jets during the Falklands war. (*Pete Warren*)

47347 leaves Dinton with the last train out of Chilmark RAF depot on 2 November 1994. The MoD shunting locos (254 and 259) had brought the wagons up from Chilmark, about 1½ miles in the distance on the right-hand track. (*Andy Read*)

(*left*) The MoD sidings at Dinton and Chilmark were home to a few industrial locos. 244 is pictured outside the sheds at Chilmark on 4 October 1992. (*Paul Abbott*)

(*right*) MoD loco 259 at RAF Chilmark facility on 4 October 1992. (*Paul Abbott*)

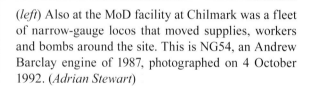

(*left*) Also at the MoD facility at Chilmark was a fleet of narrow-gauge locos that moved supplies, workers and bombs around the site. This is NG54, an Andrew Barclay engine of 1987, photographed on 4 October 1992. (*Adrian Stewart*)

(*right*) NG52, another Andrew Barclay loco (721) with a passenger coach and bomb-carrying wagons on 15 October 1987. (*Keith Usher*)

(*left*) NG52 exposes its engine on 15 October 1987. (*Keith Usher*)

Russ Ferrett

Former driver at Salisbury

The following two stories come from Russ Ferrett who started at the same time as I did. Russ and I were also made redundant together in 1975; Russ moved to Euston and I went, bizarrely, to Old Oak Common – what was I thinking! Although the work at Old Oak was actually quite good and I got a chance to work on the Westerns, having a particularly exciting trip to Birmingham and back on 1023 Western Fusilier, *lodging in London in the Old Oak Common hostel was a nightmare and it was like living in a prison except that you had a key. Both Russ and I hated it; it was no surprise that we ended up leaving the railway in 1977 to return home. I was lucky to get back on the railway at Salisbury on the footplate on 9 March 1978, all thanks to Martin Chant, the assistant depot manager, who kept me informed of any vacancies whilst I was working for Dennlings Hardware as a delivery van driver. Russ was unable to get back on the railways and now works for Hampshire Fire Brigade.*

At the age of 16, finishing secondary education and the son of an ex-train driver, there was only one career that I wished for and that was to join the railway to become a trainee driver. So on 22 July 1974 I started what was to be a short, but enjoyable, time with British Rail.

Southampton Docks had half a dozen sets of men, who crewed the docks' shunters and that was my start as a traction trainee. After only weeks I was placed on a course at Southampton Terminus that was to last nine weeks and give me all the basic and safety knowledge to ride the footplate as a secondman. Father was tracking my progress with interest and it was he who suggested that on completion of my secondman's course I should consider applying to join the links at Salisbury Motive Power Department. This I duly did and five fresh-faced young lads – colleagues Mike Pearce, Gary Pollard, Roger Luckins, Adrian Heffernen and myself – started their railway careers as junior secondmen. I was absolutely delighted with my appointment and I immediately set about finding lodgings and eventually settled well into the home of Mr and Mrs Hoskins of Manor Road, Salisbury.

In the first week of our careers at the Motive Power Department we were given spare or as/ordered turns and start times for all of us would have been in daylight hours. This allowed us to do depot familiarisation and get to know the other crew members who came and went as their rosters demanded of them. It also allowed us to sample the atmosphere of Salisbury depot, which still remains with me today: the creaky wooden stairs up to the first floor and the shiny clean drivers' cabin, so beautifully kept together by Bob Bailey who had been retired from the main line due to health problems. The sash windows that poured light into the cabin looked towards West signalbox and you could observe the 'up home' signals rising and falling throughout the day, giving you prior warning of trains approaching from Westbury and Exeter. It was only seven years since the departure of steam traction at Salisbury and in truth the depot and all of the staff was still reeling from the changes that had taken place over the last ten years or so. Drivers from other depots would come and go, adding stories of the weather, behaviour of locos and all sorts of topical issues that were the news of the day. Devonshire, Bristol, London and other regional accents were all to be heard, sometimes moaning, sometimes spreading humorous stories, and it all made a heady atmosphere for a wide-eyed 16-year-old who was relishing each day of belonging to Salisbury shed.

Russ Ferrett seen in the cab of 47347 in 1975. (*Russ Ferrett collection*)

Some characters were well known, as generally a job on the footplate was a job for life, so faces and friends from other depots would come into our drivers' room at Salisbury and immediately start a rapport with all the crew sharing the rest room. In my first week this gave witness to a most comical occurrence when a well-known Exeter driver, who was as jolly as a clown, burst into the drivers' room after working the first train up from Exeter. As soon as he found a seat, Salisbury drivers and secondmen started setting about him, teasing him about his accent, his driver's hat and the general noise that he made as he scraped his chair on the floor whilst most were talking quietly. The Exeter driver rose to the occasion, volleying at the comments with enthusiasm and a broad grin, his Devonshire accent twanging near to shouting pitch as he lit a small piece of paper on the gas water boiler so as to light the grill on the cooker for his toast. Grill alight and paper extinguished (or so he thought), disposed of into the bin and still flashing the cheerful banter across the room and being frequently verbally jostled by the Salisbury crews, he filled his tea pot with hot water and placed his butties under the grill, broadcasting that he would not share his butties with anyone. Suddenly, a cry went up that the bin was on fire, and without delay the Exeter driver leapt into action. As we all looked on, slightly anxious, he poured his fresh pot of tea into the smoking bin and extinguished the fire. Nerves quickly turned to noisy, Mickey taking shouts from the cabin full of Salisbury crews, jeering and teasing the poor old western man who had gone as red as a turkey with embarrassment. The noise and laughter was so raucous that Nobby Clark, the Shed Foreman, came in, adding his own verbal attack.

The laughter had my sides hurting and there was more to come. Whilst protesting his innocence and yearning for his lost pot of fresh tea, it was noticed to the absolute hysterics of all in the cabin that now his toasted butties had caught fire under the grill. All was lost, tea thrown away as an extinguisher, toasties burnt black, and ridicule from all around him about the cost of replacing our bin. I can remember crying with laughter and watching the poor old Exeter man concede defeat. He was rapidly offered food and a fresh pot of tea from the Salisbury crews who had enjoyed his disaster. He accepted defeat gracefully, everyone chuckled, and throughout all of this somehow he kept his hat on – for some strange reason western men always did. Southern men always thought that western men had their hat riveted on once they were promoted to driver.

A variety of stories come in unending supply to railwaymen across the network simply because of the unique and diverse pattern of work that train drivers sign up to when they choose a career on the footplate. However, I am certain that my depot, Salisbury, had a very special atmosphere with the railwaymen – in general, very decent people – and for the short time that I had there until redundancy, has enriched my life.

One of my favourite turns of duty was simply called 'up and down one o'clock'. The duty started at 05.55 and should have been to take the first train out of the bay platform calling at Dean, Dunbridge and Romsey, finally with a change of crew for a Portsmouth driver at Southampton. On this particular day the first train from Salisbury to Southampton was being used as a driver-training trip on the Hampshire unit which was the traction for that turn. The shed foreman informed driver Ron Pearcey and myself that we were to take a Class 33 Crompton light engine to Eastleigh for fuelling and then use the same loco to travel to Bevois park sidings where we would couple up to the van train in readiness to run to Clapham Junction. Ron and I dutifully prepared the Crompton and at a steady pace followed the Hampshire unit towards Romsey. After

At the annual Salisbury retirement dinner dance, retired drivers Ron Pearcey (on the left) and Tom Parsons take a rest from the excitement. Ron was a cheeky little man who never wore his false teeth; upset him and he would threaten to suck you to death! When Tom retired in 1988 I got my promotion to driver. You could near on work out when you would get your driving position. Indeed if it hadn't been for the fact that one of our drivers, Robin Cane, died whilst still at work, I would have taken my Uncle Ron's position! Tom, as many other drivers did, handed me his old equipment to carry on using, most of which I still have and use, except the single cup teapot which wore out and leaked! (*Paul Abbott*)

133

turning the tight curve at Milford just south-east of Salisbury we steadily accelerated up the bank towards Dean when Ron spotted that the diesel unit, in front of us by a few miles, had struck a pheasant and it was in the four-foot, giving its last dying throws. The brake was sharply applied and my driver said: 'Get that bird Russ, I'll have him for dinner this week'. With the now dead bird safely collected, we rattled and rolled to Eastleigh, then down to Bevois Park sidings at Southampton. After attaching to the vans we hurried them non-stop to Clapham junction where we took off the engine and ran loco only to London Waterloo. By approximately midday we were connected to our eight-coach train at Waterloo and ready to provide the 13.00 to Salisbury where we would be relieved by an Exeter driver who would take the train back to the West Country. I was only 16 or 17 years of age and so keen to be a good driver's assistant. Ron could see this so he said that I could drive the train and he would coach me all the way to Salisbury. This was quite easy to do on a Crompton as the cab had dual controls.

All went very well; I was nervous but excited as I drove the train, stopping at Woking, Basingstoke and Andover and it was on this final run down the bank towards Porton and Salisbury that Ron decided to pluck the pheasant! I can remember giggling at Ron as he coated himself in feathers. They were all over the control desk, the floor of the loco and particularly all over Ron. Waving at the signalman at Tunnel Junction we entered Salisbury Tunnel where Ron decided that if he opened the loco door behind me and the window on his (secondman's) side, the feathers could be blown out. We trundled out of the tunnel approaching East box and I could not stop chuckling. The cab of our engine resembled one of those winter scene decorations that adorn some mantlepieces at Christmas that create a snowy scene when you shake them! Instead of little white flakes looking like snow we were both completely covered in feathers and minute pieces of down. The draught through the cab had created a whirlwind of itchy, sneezy feathers and down that looked like a mini blizzard. I safely brought the train to a gentle stop at platform 4 with Ron beckoning me to go way up the platform past the waiting Exeter driver so he had time to try and brush us and the cab clean. It didn't work. I stopped just a few yards past our waiting relief driver. I will never forget the look on his face as he entered the cab of the loco with feathers still floating in the air and Ron trying to look so innocent as he blew through pouted lips (he never wore his teeth in) to try

and remove a feather from his forehead. His cheeky little face had the look of a naughty puppy that had just shredded a cushion whist his owners were out. There were feathers all over the place and particularly all over him. The relief driver could not get his words out but he was definitely mumbling expletives. Ron seized his moment when with innocent wide eyes he said: 'Engine's good, mate, eight on' and as he grabbed the now naked pheasant off of the control desk cheerily said: 'This is for my dinner, leave the door open for a while, me old mate, the draught should clear this lot out by Wilton'!

We shot off of the loco and had hardly got four or five paces down the platform when Ron absolutely cracked up with the giggles. As the train got right away and the coaches slipped by us, we waved at the guard, or rather, I waved and Ron waved his plucked, naked pheasant. The look on the Exeter guard's face said it all. Ron's trust in my capabilities and his saucy, relaxed banter will stay with me forever; the train now gone he looked at me with a half-sincere expression and said: 'You did well today, mate, but if you had gone just a bit faster through the tunnel the draught would have had those feathers out the cab.' Happy days!

Three Generations of Railway Life

by Barry Yeatman, guard at Salisbury

Demonstrating the railway's 'family feel' is this illustration from Barry Yeatman.

- Grandfather Yeatman 51 years
- Don Yeatman 51 years
- Reg Yeatman 48 years
- Ernie Yeatman 41 years
- Jack Yeatman 8 years
- Len Yeatman 42 years
- David Yeatman 2 years
- Barry Yeatman 26 years

My grandfather started work with British Rail in 1896, passing the career on to five sons and two grandsons. I will be the very last of three generations when I retire in 2015, giving the Yeatman name a total of 269 years of railway life.

6998 *Burton Agnes Hall* about to depart for Yeovil on 23 July 1988. (*Paul Abbott*)

(*beow*) 170308 waiting to go on shed at Salisbury on 5 March 2001. This unit was the last 170 at Salisbury. (*Russ Whelan*)

47709 with 47712 on the rear, visited Salisbury Traincare Depot on 14 February 2006 so that the coaching stock could be serviced after working in with the Pullman Special. (*Mike Pearce*)

(*left*) Barry Hayter, left, Don Macey, centre, and Danny Finnis. Barry, now retired, was and still is a keen gardener, often bringing in his produce for us to try; his pickled onions were superb! Don, also now retired, knew how to get the best out of any engine and you were always guaranteed an exciting run with him. Danny was an ex-GWR man but we did not hold that against him because he was a very friendly man, a joy to work with. He did not have the best of health but never complained. He sadly died before retiring. (*Andy Beavis*)

Brian Anderson was the last messenger boy to be employed by BR at Salisbury when he started his career in 1982, and looks as if he was loving every minute of it. He is now a driver at Salisbury along with his father Steve and brother Tony. (*Steve Anderson*)

Mike Wareham, left, Eddie Simms, and Hoss Smith on the platform. Mike was a keen DIYer, indeed his nickname was 'Jewson'. He nearly burnt his house down once, when using a blowtorch to remove paint from the barge boards. Eddie's nickname was 'Snoozle' as he could fall asleep anywhere but he was always a laugh and a good driver. Hoss was a well-respected guard who greeted everybody with 'Good old boy'. (*Andy Beavis*)

Steve Chislett

Station Control Point Operator at Salisbury

Before joining South West Trains I had 24 years' experience of working for bus companies in various roles, starting in 1974 as a driver and Conductor Allocation Clerk for Bristol Omnibus Company at Bath. Selected as a management trainee I learnt all aspects of the bus operation business over two years, resulting in a number of positions and finally Traffic Superintendent (Bath) until privatisation of the company in 1986. When Badgerline was formed I was appointed as Commercial Officer (Bath) until I successfully applied for a position with Wilts & Dorset as Operations Manager (Salisbury), a job that I held until I left that company in 1997.

My career in the railway industry has been relatively short, having started as a Revenue Protection Assistant based at Salisbury on Monday 22 October 2001. After a corporate welcome day at Friars Bridge Court in London and a local induction day at Southampton, full training was undertaken at Eastleigh Station in offices on platform 1. The trainer at the time was Chris D'Alcorn who had many years of training people for revenue duties and I have my 'Certificate of Training' with an 89% score dated 9 November 2001 duly signed by Chris who did all he could for those who found the training difficult. There were frequent assessments on fares, especially on reading the

Steve Chislett in Salisbury signalbox.
(*George Foster*)

bulky and heavy fares manuals that we had to carry, in addition to the Sportis ticket machine that all RPAs and commercial guards used at that time.

Duties varied, with coverage arranged to meet requirements. The earliest start was 04.55 to travel up to Grateley to 'man' the ticket hut on that station until approximately 10.00 when you would travel on the next available service as far as Andover and return to Salisbury for a 'Personal Needs Break' or PNB for short and, if I remember correctly, we then did a trip to Templecombe and back to finish the day. When a block was arranged at Waterloo any available RPAs would meet there for allocation to a team to check all tickets and passes of passengers alighting or boarding trains on their allocated platform with an amazing range of excuses being offered.

After six months as an RPA, I applied to become a commercial guard, six months being the minimum time between starting with the company and being entitled to apply for other vacancies. On 10 May 2002 I was notified that my application had been successful and after satisfying the Recruitment & Assessment Centre at St Johns Walk in Basingstoke and a personal interview, I was accepted for training as a commercial guard at Basingstoke Training Centre, starting in August 2002. The intensive training included aspects such as Personal Track Safety (PTS) qualification to enable a Safety Critical Work Identification (SCWID) card to be issued so that guard duties could be performed.

I well remember the apprehension of most of us on the course, including a number of former Salisbury RPA colleagues, at stepping over the live conductor rail carrying 650 volts DC electric current. Use of the 'short circuit' bar, too, was quite dramatic just outside Waterloo station where we learnt how to isolate a section of conductor rail in an emergency with a flash and a crackle – pop! Other practical skills learnt during the course covered the use of track circuit clips after derailment, ensuring that you didn't attach one end of the clip onto the live 'juice' rail and fry yourself in the process. Quite a number of days were spent 'banging and clanging' in Clapham Yard, attaching and detaching air hoses and electrical jumper leads between slam-door, third-rail, electric multiple units (EMUs), often referred to as 400s or 'juicers'. Although it was hard work acting as guard on these trains you definitely felt that you had earned your wages.

My first day as a fully-fledged commercial guard involved me working the 17.28 from Waterloo to Basingstoke with an unknown driver from Fratton Depot near Portsmouth. He collected the 12-coach train from Clapham Yard and brought it to Waterloo and after winding the headcode blinds to red to act as the tail lamp for the journey to Basingstoke, he had a quick word with me about passengers leaving all the doors open at certain stations and how he resolved this quickly to save time. On arrival at said station I requested passengers to close the doors behind them on the 'Loudaphone' system, but despite the request a high proportion of the many doors were left open. As discussed with him at Waterloo, I stood in his view on the platform and indicated that all passengers had alighted. He then put the train in reverse, stopped abruptly, closing all the doors facing in one direction, then put the train in forward, and again stopped sharply, closing all the doors facing the other direction. Job done with minimum effort!

After passing the relevant guards' assessments and exams I was authorised to work on the 400s (EMUs) and Class 159 diesel multiple units (DMUs) that were new in 1994, 3-coach units that could be joined together to form a maximum length train of nine coaches. Additional tuition was received to operate the new Class 170 2-coach units that were self-contained so that if there was a 'hybrid' train with a mix of Class 159 and 170

units the guard was unable to patrol the entire length of the train without alighting at a station. Whatever train I worked on as a commercial guard was always pleasant and enjoyable so it was a great disappointment when my health required me to be redeployed. Fortunately, I was transferred in September 2005 to work the Customer Information System (CIS) in the Salisbury signalbox. A great team spirit exists between the signallers, and what is now called the Station Control Point (SCP). With good communication, operating difficulties are dealt with effectively, causing minimum disruption to services. Occasionally, however, major disruption does occur, when personal announcements are used rather than the pre-recorded ones, to keep passengers updated.

It is always very reassuring to hear Steve's personal announcements whenever things do go wrong!

Salisbury was home depot to the South West Trains route-learning DMU 960012 *John Cameron*, ex W55028. It is pictured in 7 road being re-fuelled and having the final drives and oil levels checked after route-learning duties from Salisbury to Westbury-Castle Cary-Yeovil Pen Mill in September 2007. (*Chris Pelling*)

(*left*) Sandite unit 'Ben', ex-W55025, seen inside Salisbury Traincare Depot where it is having fresh supplies of sandite loaded on board in October 1994. (*Willy Ameanu*)

(*below*) On 21 March 2009 Salisbury's resident bubble car 960012 was moved to its new home at Swanage where it is seen just after arrival being pressed straight into use on a Swanage Railway members' day special after the failure of their 08 loco. (*Mark Pike*)

Donna's Railway Story

by Donna Pollard (née Ridgewell), a driver at Salisbury

Donna now explains how she ended up becoming Salisbury's second female driver.

Having made 'Kiss me Quick' hats at Southend, flipped burgers at Burger King and spent many nights pea picking, I decided I really should do something more worthwhile with my life. I got a job at the Ford Motor Company at the age of 18, fitted 523 oil and water pumps a day for a couple of years then was promoted to Statistical Process Control Coordinator – that's 'Quality Control Inspector' to you and me. Being young and ambitious I fancied being self-employed and making my millions in Network Marketing. I was doing rather well; packed up work to concentrate on my new enterprise but then the company it was based around went bust. Now for the railway connections ...

I passed my 'Knowledge Test' and became a taxi driver in Thurrock, working on my own, mainly picking up off the railway station taxi ranks. This quickly evolved into a company with several drivers working for me with my family running the office and book keeping. We took on a large account for British Rail, transporting people and goods all over the country. Unfortunately, we were only a small business with little capital and could not sustain BR's way of dealing with accounts! I took a full time job in the *Railway Tavern* public house as a barmaid. Without the taxi business to run I now had time to concentrate more on my favourite pastime, my dogs. I attended training classes twice a week with my three German Shepherds and showed them for obedience and fun classes most Sundays through the summer. Unfortunately, the bar work didn't pay too well and I started to struggle to maintain my car and buy petrol. It was at this time that a friend, who I met at the dog club, suggested that I could apply for a guard's job at Waterloo. He was a driver there and had heard there were some vacancies. At my interview I was asked what ambitions I may have for my future on the railway. I said I wouldn't mind being a driver. Sandra Williams took a dim view of this and I thought I'd blown it.

But no, I joined the railway and started the Trainman G course in September 1997. After just 12 months on the railway I found myself being interviewed for a driver's job – by Sandra Williams and Richard Trellis. I had applied for Bournemouth, Weymouth and Salisbury (in that order of preference). As the 11-hour driver's day plus three hours travelling to and from Essex would have been too much and as I didn't want to live any closer to London it was best to move away completely. Richard Trellis talked extensively about Bournemouth depot which pleased me as I was already familiar with the town and knew my way around. At the end of my last day as a guard I went to see my guard standards manager as I had not received any joining instructions for the school. We went to the offices on the raft at Waterloo where the papers were being faxed through. I watched the paper come through and it was headed 'Trainee driver Salisbury'. I said rather loudly: 'Salisbury, where the hell is that?' The entire raft went silent. 'Is that not what you were expecting', asked the GSM? I explained that I believed I was going to Bournemouth. It was left that I would start at the school on Monday and that someone would be in touch to sort it out. And so I started the driver 2000 course in September 1998.

During the first morning's tea break I received a phone call from Bob Silk, driver standards manager at Salisbury. He had heard of my reaction to the news that I was going to Salisbury and wanted to sort it out. Having had the weekend to think about it, I'd decided that if I was to be moving to the other side of the country on my own that it really didn't matter where it was. Bob was happy with that and so Salisbury it would be. Having commuted from Essex to Basingstoke for three months whilst attending the training school I was given the news that in January I would be starting with my driver instructor at Salisbury. I knew that this meant I would have to move. With a house to be sold in Essex and no spare cash I hadn't really planned for this day so on the Sunday I boarded a train in Stanford-le-Hope to set out on the three-hour journey to Salisbury.

I arrived at Salisbury station at 9.00pm, stood on the platform and hoped that the hotel across the road had a vacancy. I booked in for three nights, as that was all I could afford to pay in advance. On Monday morning I was to meet with my driver instructor, Bill Rillstone, for the first time. I had been warned that he didn't care too much for women on the railway, disliked 'Waterloo' people and was none too keen on ex-guards in the driver's grade. This was going to be good! I was about to become the second woman driver at Salisbury and was not expecting much in the way of help. In addition, I was one of five trainees at the depot – the first batch for many years. I met with Bill and we got on rather well. His wife always packed extra cake in his lunchbox for me and he even arranged for me to lodge at his daughter's house. Bill would pick me up for work each day and take me home at the end of the shift – unless I wanted to go shopping of course!

I finished my hours with Steve Anderson, but 10 years later, I still hear Bill's voice in my head in times of need on the track – giving instructions or advice on how to, why and when.

The driver of the Thames train that was involved in the Paddington crash passed out as a driver at the same time as me and I suddenly felt very blessed for all those hours I had spent listening to other drivers' experiences and reasons for certain behaviours and methods of driving. I also feel very privileged to have had the opportunity to 'route learn' with Fred Beavis, Alfie Fletcher and the likes, before they retired.

In November 1999, I found myself involved in an incident that was not of my making. Still being a 'green', 'boil in the bag', 'outsider', 'woman' driver, I wondered what sort of reaction I would get from my colleagues at the depot. To my delight, I received unprecedented support from the 'new' to the 'most experienced' of drivers. From this point I felt that Salisbury was my new home. When I moved to Salisbury in 1998 in search of a better life I didn't know what a pheasant looked like so imagine my surprise when I met my husband – over a dead one!

My train terminated at Yeovil Junction and I was booked to await the empties from Honiton to attach to my train before driving empty stock back to Salisbury. The driver of the Honiton portion shunted across to platform 2 where I – a nervous post-qualifier – waited anxiously for him to attach to my unit. When the train stopped and the driver opened the end door, I saw that I knew him only as a Salisbury driver instructor; we exchanged a polite 'hello' and he proceeded to attach to my unit. After the first failed attempt of getting a brake release he split the units and 'banged them together' a bit harder. Being the new driver, I was thinking I must have done something wrong and was getting rather anxious, as I had never had problems attaching before. Again we were unsuccessful in getting a brake release so after a further attempt we decided we really ought to have a good look at the couplings to see what was going on. To our dismay, there was a pheasant squashed into the coupling which had now been rammed in further with our three attempts at coupling up and was now also occupying every pin of the electrical box. It took us 15 minutes to pull the carcass clear and successfully attach the units together. We had an eventless trip back to Salisbury where I met with the other driver to put our reports in to the supervisor. This is where I found out his name and held my first real conversation with him.

You could say the rest is history but when Gary proposed to me, I had to say yes for one really good reason – to get the BR free travel boxes – which he actually presented to me on the Top Table during our wedding speeches!

Salisbury drivers, and husband and wife, Donna Ridgewell and Gary Pollard on 30 October 2005. (*Gary Pollard collection*)

(*above*) Salisbury Railway FC just before playing Bulford FC, c.October 1988. From left to right, back row: Steve Doyle (plumber), Mike Pearce (driver), Dave Wilson (shunter), Mark Freeman (postman), Ian Mundy (depot technician), Derek Pearce (guard), Nick Swift (dust cart driver), Dave Lloyd (S&T and team manager); front row: John Doyle (student), Paul Vincent (railman), Jock Tilly (SAS), Mick Milward (team captain, club chairman and MoD spy), Simon Pughe (top goal scorer and then shunter), Paul Evens (TV repair man), Nigel Pearce (guard), John Hill Jnr (driver for Freightliner). The railway team won 2-1 with goals from Simon Pughe and Mike Pearce. (*Julie Hill*)

(*below*) On 2 July 2005 Deltic 55019 *Royal Highland Fusilier* sneaked onto the fuel point at Salisbury CET, piloted in by Fragonset Merlin driver Adrian Stewart. (*Adrian Stewart collection*)

Our Journey Together

by Jonathan and Jacqueline Roberts of Gillingham (Dorset), regular passengers to Waterloo

A growing number of commuters and students get on at Gillingham for Salisbury, Home Counties towns or London. You can now travel the 105¼ miles and be in London by 7:40 in the morning, if you catch the 5:37. It's a long day but what makes it do-able is the railway experience in air-conditioned, commuter-type trains and, above all, with the friendliness of the train crew and trolley stewards. Passengers, too, are a bit different if starting west of Basingstoke – we expect to find seats, and though it's a squeeze on peak trains as they fill up towards London, the rugby scrum tactics around doors aren't a feature of the West of England line; time is valued by comfort not by egg-timer standards. You only have to listen to the welcoming noises as regulars board the 5:37! There's also the perk of finding 'our' train at Waterloo – listen for the sound of the underfloor diesel engines, and there's normally no problem about finding the right platform. This usually guarantees a bit of extra comfort before starting westwards. Travel can be a real pleasure, cruising through the Vale of Wardour or over Salisbury Plain, especially beautiful in spring and autumn as colours change in the fields and trees. A downside is the recent arrival of 'digital Doris', the automated on-train announcer who is too loud and says too much for her own good. More than one Salisbury driver calls her Sonya, because she gets onyer nerves!

It's actually the Gillingham to Waterloo line that's responsible for me meeting my wife. I'm a political consultant with a London desk, while Jacqueline is a physiotherapist with a practice in Dorset and in Harley Street. We tend to work long hours, so the first morning train (that 5:37 again at Gillingham!) or the last one or two of the evening (the 20:20 or 21:20 from Waterloo) are often our necessary if not favourite trains. However, I always preferred the country-end coach, while Jacqueline was used to the middle coach of the 3-car set. So while we had both commuted since 1997, it took until 2002 for a first encounter. We can pinpoint this precisely to 5 December 2002 on the 20:35 from Waterloo, with unit 159002 going beyond Salisbury. I had been to a Japanese evening class and Jacqueline to an Italian one. We were sitting diagonally opposite each other.

When the trolley turned up, I offered to buy a cup of tea. Jacqueline offered to buy tea the following month. Just a second chance encounter, because my dotting around the clock with train times meant there was no consistency about meeting. Sometimes three or six months would go by, and generally it was two rather work-weary individuals who would spot each other on a late train back, and talk about recent events and future plans. But there was definitely pleasure in chatting ...

One evening, Jacqueline (a divorcee, I later found out) was met at Gillingham by a tall dark stranger, who whisked her off to Mere, so that somewhat dampened any aspirational thoughts of mine. (It turned out to have been her father!) By 2005, we were still meeting on an unplanned basis, but the chats were definitely more extensive. On 12 May, we met on the 20:20, myself full of plans for the plane flight the following day to Slovenija, where I was looking to buy a house. I nearly said more in the Gillingham station car park where we said goodbye, but didn't.

Nine miles later I was in a major collision with a tractor on the B3081, and helicoptered to Frenchay Hospital in Bristol with a broken leg, pelvis, ribs etc, for an emergency operation. Months passed in recuperation until I resumed commuting, on crutches, on 5 September, initially avoiding the morning peak trains, so not seeing Jacqueline. However I caught the 5:37 that Thursday, and Jacqueline was there. She was shocked by the change, and it has to be that day that our lives began to be pulled closer together.

Various other encounters on the West of England trains cemented that process over the following months. On Saturday 15 October, I was going to Northampton Rugby Club on the 8:42 from Gillingham, and was surprised to see Jacqueline, who was running an AGM of St Thomas's Hospital Physiotherapy Association. The encounter was all great fun, even though I was enlisted to help her with the preparatory paperwork.

On another occasion, still stick-bound and having difficulty with sitting, I had been offered an upgrade to first class by a kind guard, Dave Tattam. He alerted Jacqueline that I was there. Apparently she shot back up to see me, and was delighted that the female sitting opposite me alighted at Andover! Where were things leading?

In March 2006 I was still limping badly. I turned up for the 5:37 on Thursday 16th and asked Jacqueline which train she was catching that evening; we arranged to meet on the 20:20. On the train back she asked me what I was doing about my limp, and I asked if she could provide some physiotherapy. A session was booked for 30 March, which was a start to definite improvement. A further session was arranged for Thursday 6 April, and this turned out to be our Waterloo! Arriving there very early for the 20:20, we decided to go to the Bonaparte bar for a drink. A return via the Pasty Shop along the concourse, and on to 159002 (again) at the buffers, with Mike Brown the guard and Richard Owen on the Exeter trolley. Mike commented to Jacqueline as we boarded: 'Who's your hanger on?' We were in full chat as we progressed westward.

I had suggested at the bar that we should go to see Monet's garden at Giverny in Normandy. Somewhere between Basingstoke and Andover, we were looking up possible dates for our trip, when suddenly the lightning struck. 'Are you feeling the same as I am?', I asked Jacqueline. There wasn't any need for words, it was in her eyes. The rest of the journey passed in hugs and kisses.

We were engaged ten days later. A number of South West Trains' staff came to our wedding in September – which had a railway theme. We walked down the aisle in Milton Clevedon church to 'Coronation Scot' (which starts with a train whistle); the wedding cake was six feet long and decorated as 159002 at Gillingham (we cut it at seats 5 and 6 in First Class where our lives had changed); the front seats had SWT reservations (thank you, you know who); there were train chocolates, ticket place cards, and a poem about that wonderful journey on 6 April (which I'd written that July).

Late in 2007 we saw that the original 159.0 series trains were being refurbished. Jacqueline had the brilliant idea of phoning Salisbury depot to see what would happen to the seats – we agreed that we should try to save 'our seats' if that was possible. The depot manager was Lisa Hindley, who admitted she was a romantic. She would see what was possible. In due course, the answer came back – yes you are welcome to the seats, but would we mind if there was a bit of publicity for the depot and the line? We were really delighted with the kind response, and were happy to have a photo taken.

We thought we would probably have to hire a van and collect the seats from the depot. However we guessed that things were moving up the scale when we were asked which train we might choose to board at Gillingham for a handover at Waterloo, and when it was suggested that a few journalists might be there! It turned out that the 07:16 from Gillingham wouldn't be right as there wouldn't be enough room for the TV crews from Salisbury ...

It was the 07:44 for us, on 12 February 2008 – intriguingly close to Valentine's Day. We'd offered to give a donation to the Railway Children charity, which is supported widely within the railway industry, and so it transpired that Jacqueline and myself were interviewed at Gillingham, on the train up to Waterloo (in 159002 newly refurbished, with Dave Thomas driving us to Salisbury and Dave Tattam as guard all the way!), changed into wedding outfit in a Portakabin on platforms 5/6 at Waterloo, and met the SWT Engineering Director, and Gordon Pettitt, a Railway Children trustee and former Director of Network South East, along with massed TV crews, reporters, and several hectic days of media coverage, which finally extended over several weeks with radio interviews and coverage as far as Peru, the United States and Eastern Europe. The seats are now in our sitting room – the window is on the same side as in the train – and we often sit in them and have a toast to our good fortune.

It is great to hear that sometimes our costumers get a little bit more than just a good journey. I would like to thank Jonathan and Jacqueline for sharing their story and wish them continued happiness together. We have many regular travellers on our line and they are a special bunch; they are very knowledgeable on their route and understand the complexity of working a single-line main line, being very tolerant when delays occur on it. I hope they realise we are proud of our 'West of England' line and try to do our best!

(*previous page*) Jacqueline and Jonathan Roberts en route to Waterloo on 12 February 2008 to take possession of their pair of original seats from a Class 159 diesel multiple unit.

(*right*) Having changed into their wedding outfits, they sit happily in their new possessions. (*both photographs Jonathan Roberts collection*)

Matt Hurst

Mobile Operations Manager at Salisbury

When things do go wrong in our area who are you gonna call? Young Matt!

I have always had an interest in railways ever since my dad became a shareholder, lifetime member and working volunteer of the Mid Hants Railway. Many a Saturday was spent travelling between Alresford and Ropley originally and then through to Medstead & Four Marks and Alton.

When I started senior school in Romsey in 1984 I quickly made friends who shared my passion for railways and over the next few years we, the intrepid six, travelled the length and breadth of the country, clocking the mileage and recording our sightings.

Four of us, however, went on to college where Business Studies was the chosen subject but after this we went our separate ways. One to the police force, one to a bank, one to British Rail and I into the freight industry. I initially joined a freight forwarder but moved in 1995 to a container shipping line based in Southampton Docks. These were good years but then in 1999 the shipping line moved to Felixstowe and the office closed with its customer base transferred to Canary Wharf. I was then left with a choice; move to London or look for a new career. It was at this stage that an opportunity to join the railway materialised.

Freightliner in Millbrook was after a Contracts Manager to oversee the daily business of its smaller clients and assist with train planning. In May that year my railway career began and, would you believe it, one of my first tasks was to create an outbased Contracts Manager office within a shipping line's premises in London's Docklands. On returning to Southampton, promotion to Customer Services Manager beckoned. I now became the Contract Manager's manager. This was when I realised two things. Firstly, that sitting behind a desk really was not for me and, secondly, that I should have joined the railway a long time ago.

In 2002 Railtrack ran an open event in Guildford for staff wishing to join them as Field Managers. I duly went along and, liking what I heard, put my name forward and received an interview. There began a long wait to hear if I had been successful. Then, one day, a letter saying congratulations, you have a job at Eastleigh. Little did I know that they had made a clerical error. They had appointed two people to one job so no sooner had I started than I was displaced. Very soon, however, my Operations Delivery Manager, Geoff Norman, asked if I would like to join the team in Salisbury? I thought long and hard about it (about 30 seconds actually) and said yes, so, in May 2003 I joined the team. After spending a few days getting to know the area I received a call on a Sunday morning from the signaller in Salisbury. At last, what I had been trained for; my first 'shout' but what could it be? A dead peacock in Tisbury loop! Thus started a diverse and interesting career.

Since arriving in Salisbury the job title has changed from Field Manager to Mobile Operations Manager; even the company name has changed to Network Rail but the role and objectives of the MOM remain the same. I've also had the ability to diversify within the role including spells with British Transport Police patrolling the network during school holidays and, more recently, being trained as an observer for the Network Rail helicopter programme – a role that I generally love but sometimes regret (especially in rough weather!).

The main day-to-day role hasn't changed, however. It has been known for a call to come through from the signallers stating that my assistance is required to prevent an emergency. The same adrenalin that pumped on that first Sunday returns. What could it be? A points failure, a level crossing failure, a train in trouble or kids mucking around? No, it usually involves a trip to the chilled cabinet at Tesco to obtain milk for the signallers' tea or, if a serious emergency is developing, to purchase and deliver ice cream to the panel.

One particular incident that I vividly recall happened earlier this year (2009) when the south of England experienced the worst snow storms for nearly two decades. Although Salisbury is not immune to the weather, all staff pulled together to ensure that the intrepid travellers got home to their loved ones. That may well be the theory but on Tuesday 3 February I was working the late shift and listening to the ever worsening problems being experienced throughout the area. Reports were being received continuously. Firstly the A30 was closed due to an accident in the snow, then the A338 for the same reason and finally the A36 because vehicles were unable to climb Pepperbox Hill. This effectively closed my last route home so the only option left was to catch the train. After parking the Network Rail truck and ensuring that the office was locked I made my way back to the station to catch the last train to Portsmouth at 22.34. The train was slightly late because of the worsening weather but at least it was definitely running, emphasising the statement that all staff do their best to ensure that intrepid travellers get home.

On arriving at the station the signaller, John Say, advised me that there were two points failures at Salisbury station effectively trapping the service to Chandler's Ford. The S&T department were working on one set of points but my assistance was requested to look at the other. Knowing that my train was late I agreed and made my way to the London end of the station and, sure enough, these points would not lock and would need to be clipped and plugged. A number of

trains were requiring access to or from the station area. Firstly, a train out of platform 6; then one into platform 4 and finally one out of platform 2. When I asked which train was needing to exit platform 2 he said: 'If I tell you, you'll get upset!' Shortly after, I stood aside only to see my last train to Romsey disappear into the blizzard like snow. Thanks John! (*I was the announcer on duty that night and I can personally verify all that Matt says is absolutely true but was John laughing or was it a sign of concern for one of his colleagues? Maybe, we'll never know! – Steve Chislett*)

All joking aside, the role can be stressful and traumatic but the camaraderie between the staff at Salisbury means that the job, however big or small, can be done in a professional, friendly and efficient way.

On 5 June 2008 159107 proceeds at 5mph through flood water at Gillingham where there has always been a problem with flooding despite new drainage being installed. This is the kind of incident Matt Hurst would be called out to attend. (*Gary Pollard*)

Leaking as much steam as a steam engine is 7007 on a Portsmouth to Cardiff train in Salisbury platform on 3 March 1963. (*Pete Warren*)

Salisbury Traincare Depot

We now bring the story up to date with a look at Salisbury Traincare Depot. The depot personnel do a grand job of looking after our trains and compared to 158 units owned by other train operating companies our 159 look far superior and are running as well today as they did when they were new.

Salisbury's new £7.5m Traincare Depot that took 17 weeks to design and a further 52 weeks to build was handed over in December 1992 by the contractors Geoffrey Osborne, who had worked under the direction of BR's network civil engineer, to the then depot manager Nick Horton. The site, however, did not officially open for service until Friday 11 June 1993 when an elaborate opening ceremony was put on, using two 159 units entering the service shed together to the strains of Elgar's *Pomp and Circumstance March No.4* and accompanied by a laser light show. The then Bishop of Salisbury, the Right Rev John Austin Baker, blessed the depot and the assembled guests, who included Sir Bob Reid (BR chairman), Peter Field (Network South East divisional director), Brian Everard (Osborne managing director), Simon Jones (BR network civil engineer project manager), Selwyn Dixon (BR project engineer), leading dignitaries from Salisbury and other communities along the line,

depot management and staff, who all then enjoyed a celebratory meal.

From December 1992 the 159 units started running on ghost rosters between Salisbury and Basingstoke to acquire mileage reliability testing. On 22 February 1993 unit 159004 worked the first through working from Waterloo to Exeter leaving Salisbury at 08.30 as 2Z12, later departing Waterloo at 10.15 as 2Z13 and Exeter at 14.42 as 2Z14. This was booked as a timing run for train planning but, unfortunately, on the day the unit suffered an engine problem on the 57 car and as a result ran from Basingstoke to Exeter and Salisbury on just two of the three engines; this ruined the timing run but showed that a unit was capable of running on just two engines over the switchback route, achieving a creditable 54mph up Honiton bank. A unit running well on three engines runs normally at around 71mph, with best speeds of 77mph. In comparison, a Class 50 with nine coaches could maintain roughly the same; Class 47/7 65mph to 72mph, Class 33 35mph to 40mph. A week later on 3 March and in full working order, 159004 worked the first official public passenger train when it conveyed councillors and invited members of the press and public between Exeter and Honiton. Throughout the rest of March 159 units started to enter public service.

The GWR goods shed that was in Salisbury Fisherton Yard. It had just been vacated by the exhibition train company and was due for demolition to make way for the 159 depot. (*Derek Pearce*)

A general view of the Salisbury Traincare Depot under construction in April 1992. (*Steve Anderson*)

South Western Turbos are Coming, May 1992, complete with apostrophe. (*Steve Anderson*)

The interior of the depot whilst under construction in May 1992. (*Steve Anderson*)

On Saturday 26 June 1993 Chris Heaps sponsored a special high-speed run with a view to breaking the one-hour running time record between Waterloo and Salisbury. The manufacturer and Network South East allowed the normal 90mph limit of the unit to rise to 99mph.

At 10.45 1Z10 left Waterloo platform 12 formed of unit 159003 and with Salisbury driver Mike Cullen in control. Clapham was passed in 5mins 7secs, Woking in 19mins 20secs, Basingstoke 34mins 2secs, 99mph being reached at Farnborough, Hook and mile post 78, and arrival at Salisbury was in 59 minutes. The unit averaged 92.6mph between Surbiton and milepost 78 with an overall average of 85mph and all on the day were pleased and driver Cullen was duly praised for a very professional performance (drivers at Salisbury were slightly disappointed in driver Cullen as we all knew that he, if anyone, would break the one-hour barrier!).

Saturday 10 July 1993 (36 years after steam finished) was to be the last day of loco-hauled trains with the 17.45 Waterloo to Yeovil Junction the last service, hauled by 47702. Monday 12 July saw Class 159 units working all services. The last unit to arrive at Salisbury Traincare Depot was 159019 in late July 1993.

One year later, the depot received the first of many awards when fleet manager Mac MacKintosh presented the depot with an International Standard for Quality, ISO 9002. This was accepted by fitter Ray Fulford, who had worked at the old steam shed, on behalf of all his work colleagues.

Salisbury Traincare Depot has maintained high standards throughout, under the successive leadership of depot managers Nick Horton, John Parsons and current manageress Lisa Hindley, and has for the last four years in a row won the Golden Spanner industry award which is given to the best performing diesel fleet.

Peter Beale, Production Manager, has supplied the following information.

The depot now employs 101 staff:
  20 skilled technicians
  30 semi-skilled technicians
  1 depot maintenance technician
  24 train cleaners
  4 depot cleaners
  4 stores operators
  3 technical support staff
  4 production managers
  4 planning managers
  3 administration staff
  Technical performance manager
  Stores manager
  Depot manager
  Reliability engineer

Depot facilities include:
  Three-road servicing shed
  Cleaning shed
  Lifting shed
  CET and emergency fuelling facility
  Berthing for 17 units
  New fuelling shed for 2009

The current fleet consists of:
  22 Class 159 3-car units
   8 Class 159/1 3-car units
  11 Class 158 2-car units

In an average month a 3-car unit will receive approximately 95 man hours' maintenance. The depot spends around £7m on diesel fuel annually and the depot cleaners will remove over 40kgs of drinks cans and 3,280kgs of newspapers in a typical week!

Unit 159002 *City of Salisbury* consists of coaches 52874-58719-57874. Its build date was 15 June 92, and it came in service on 15 June 1993. This unit was one of the first to arrive at Salisbury and spent the first year accumulating reliability mileage; it has now covered over 2,980,000 miles and has had its engines, transmission and running gear replaced six times. Compare this to a West Country steam loco that on average completed only 1,000,000 miles, some much less.

In the course of one week 159002 will have covered between 4,500 and 5,000 miles depending on allocated diagrams and consumed in the region of 3,000 gallons of diesel fuel. It will have received seven overnight cleans and 14 station cleans, and will have been through the carriage washer at least six times. More than 50 different drivers will have driven it and 8,000 to 10,000 passengers will have ridden in it.

Inside the then new Salisbury Traincare Depot on 23 February 1993 is 159004 with 159002 in the background. (*Robin Coles*)

159001 (nearest the camera), 159002 and 159004 inside the new shed in March 1993. (*Steve Anderson*)

The middle car (58 car) of unit 159001 being examined after being the first derailment in the depot in March 1993. (*Steve Anderson*)

Fred Johnson

Retired fireman, driver and traction trainer at Salisbury

Finally we hear from Fred Johnson with some amazing revelations on a distinguished career. Fred's stories have been transcribed virtually word for word.

<u>Depot</u> Salisbury Steam, Cherry Orchard Lane, Salisbury
<u>Date</u> Wed 1 July 1948
Driver A. Morrish, Fireman F. Johnson
<u>Turn</u> 4.00pm late turn Carriage Shunter
Loco Drummond Tank No.675

Driver Morrish was known as Bud. He lived in the Lower Bemerton area, and was finishing his last years in the carriage shunting link, age of probably 61-63 years.

The turn consisted of shunting terminating trains at East and West Carriage Sidings and detaching or attaching passenger vans and/or coaches to various trains on up and down lines.

Whilst awaiting the next movement the crew with the locomotive were waiting in No.6 bay, under control of Salisbury East box. Bud was talking in general and then brought up had I heard of the Boat Train crash which occurred on 1 July 1906, 42 years ago today. Of course everyone on the railway had heard and knew a little of this. Bud then revealed some very interesting information about it to me. He was on duty, working in the vicinity of the derailment.

He informed me that he was sent in to the derailed locomotive through the front window to ascertain that the driver and fireman were dead. He was selected to do this as he was of very slim build, and was only just over five foot in height, so he could get through onto the footplate. He was now not very tall, but obviously was somewhat stouter than he was. Later that evening the bodies of the driver and fireman were the last to be removed, and this was via the locomotive window.

On reflection probably few people had known what Bud had actually done. Something that he relayed to me 40 years after the event, and 100 years on is actually being written down, no doubt a true event that had happened.

Next it was back to working action down behind the down train in platform 4, to carry on with the shunting duties.

The view from the steps down to Fisherton Street looking towards London, by Fisherton Street Bridge (up side). It shows the devastating results of the 1906 crash. The old milk dock platform is in the background, where the Railway Social Club now stands. (*Colin Hall collection*)

Depot Salisbury Steam, Cherry Orchard Lane, Salisbury
<u>Main Line Link</u> Driver A. Cambray (Bert), Fireman F. Johnson

Introduction

Bert was always very clean and smart and always wore a black dicky bow and a white stiff collar.

Having at this time in the main line link 12 weekly rotating turns, Bert had a big following of people who rode down in trains he worked, especially from Waterloo to Salisbury. They were always waiting at Waterloo armed with tape recorders and stopwatches to follow the journey. Speed restrictions were in the main ignored by him, and some very high speeds were attained, which put the *Mallard* record of 126mph in the shade. It seemed go as fast as you can, full time. On normal journeys down from Waterloo the regulator controlling steam to the cylinders would be open continuously at some point and not closed until approaching Broken Cross Bridge. The semaphore distant signal for Tunnel Junction signalbox would be seen first by the fireman who would either shout 'Right' if off or 'On' if caution. If 'On' a full emergency brake application would be made in order to stop at Tunnel Junction stop signals.

On arrival at Salisbury, time and time over, the chaps who rode down in the train with their stopwatches would come up and say to Bert: 'You were doing 140 – 142 – 144mph over a one-mile stretch between Amesbury

Junction and Porton'. And make no mistake they knew where every ¼ post per mile was and how to calculate speed. Bert's reply when they told him this was: 'Don't you print that anywhere' and would laugh it off after.

The speedometer fitted on locomotives – Merchant Navy, West Country class, etc. – only went to 100mph, and many times these went past this to no man's land so speed could not be seen on the actual loco.

I logged a selection of journeys as fireman to Bert which are hopefully of some interest to readers.

Salisbury Steam. On 1.38pm, 11 October 1960
Up Atlantic Coast Express. Arrived Salisbury 2.03pm. Departed 2.09pm. Locomotive 35016. The up journey to Waterloo went well, steam plenty. Due to arrive at Waterloo at 3.29pm, actual arrival 3.28pm. This account is logged for the later occurrence at Nine Elms depot and downward journey. Usual complaint was forthcoming from buffet staff, all coffees wasted coming round curve under Battledown flyover. Speed here was always in the region of 90mph, on up journey. After removal of train, locomotive taken light loco to Nine Elms depot at 3.57pm. Arriving on Pit Road at depot at 4.15pm. Loco number reported to foreman (Bert, short chap with cloth cap) who also had an assistant known as the foreman's runner, this man being Jim Rebbeck.

Crew then adjourned to engineman's mess room, wash up, make the tea and have tea break.

35028 *Clan Line* seen entering the single-line section at Wilton with a test run prior to the steam specials of 1986. This was a run for the Salisbury drivers to familiarise themselves with steam again, which took about five minutes! (*Keith Usher*)

Just after 5.00pm it was out to prepare the locomotive for the down service, locomotive 34068 just inside Nine Elms shed, roughly middle part.

Time off shed was 6.30pm to work 7.00pm fast to Exeter, as far as Salisbury, arrive Salisbury 8.25pm.

On arrival on the locomotive, not one tool or piece of equipment was on the locomotive. No other locomotives were handy. Bert said: 'Right, don't do anything until this engine is equipped' and off we go to see the foreman. Bert to foreman: 'No tools or equipment on that loco; when you fully equip it we will prepare it.' Foreman: 'OK'.

Bert and myself then went back and sat on the locomotive, and he said: 'When they equip us we will start our work; until then sit on the seat'. This we both did. I did glance in the firebox and there was a good fire to put over the box.

We waited and waited, no tools or anyone came near us.

It must have been somewhere approaching nearly 6.20pm when Bert said: 'I'll go and tell him we are still waiting on tools and equipment'. I walked over with him and he calmly said to the foreman that we are still awaiting our tools and have not started preparation yet.

Don't ask – all hell let loose. The assistant foreman went up a loft: tools and equipment, new or reconditioned, came down; drivers and firemen to assist us came from all directions. Bert was now in no particular hurry; we prepared loco, went out and took coal and filled water tank, and eventually were ready to leave depot at 7.00pm, and went to engine line. Left to go to Waterloo and arrived on train. Coupled. Guard informed us load 13 – 424 tons. The usual large crowd of followers were present to ride down on train, fully equipped with tape recorders, stopwatches, etc.

Signal at Waterloo platform 11 changed to green light – MT displayed in indicator – Right Away given. Time 7.16pm – 16 minutes late.

Train departs perfect and Bert sets them well alight at Vauxhall, above line speed; to Clapham, no ease down even of regulator, well over line speed. Locomotive steaming well, good job it was, and before you almost knew it past Surbiton, then Woking, all signals clear. Shovelling coal almost non-stop, past Basingstoke, Worting, slight ease down towards Enham, speedo of clock at 100mph. Through Andover and up bank to Grately and past as though the bank did not exist. Down towards Salisbury, never been so fast. The regulator was closed approaching Broken Cross Bridge as Tunnel Junction distant was spotted by me, it was clear – shouted to Bert 'Right', slight braking at Tunnel Junction and braking down for Salisbury East, but all signals clear.

Run into platform 4 and stopped for water at far end. Time 8.23pm – two minutes early.

One of the band of Bert's followers in the train said to him: 'You were doing 144mph over one mile from Amesbury Junction down. Bert's usual reply: 'Don't you print that'.

Needless to say, the rest of the week at Nine Elms depot, the loco to prepare for our train down was fully equipped with tools, etc.

35006 *Peninsular & Oriental S.N.Co*, a Salisbury engine, seen racing through Porton. (*George Lynam collection*)

Salisbury Steam. August Bank Holiday Monday 1961
Relieved Nine Elms crew, platform 11 at Waterloo station at 10.45am on locomotive 35010 Merchant Navy class to work the Atlantic Coast Express – 11.00am from Waterloo to Salisbury (engine through to Exeter). This was a non-stop train to Salisbury due to arrive at 12.23pm. Load 13 coaches – 423 tons.

It was noted from condition of this locomotive that it had recently been overhauled at Eastleigh Works. The fire door was pegged wide open and it was noted a large fire had been made – which was red hot. The safety valves were whimpering steam with the steam pressure gauge showing just short of 250 lbs per sq. inch.

Although this was a bank holiday a considerable number of enthusiasts were present at Waterloo to travel down on this service. Starting signal was cleared to green at 10.59am with indicator MT displayed. Train given Right Away and departed 11.00am – right time.

The train was started away without any slip and speed increased at a very fast rate. Past Vauxhall, then Clapham in about five minutes at a speed of over 60mph.

The steam pressure gauge never moved even with the injector on to maintain boiler water and the further we went the faster we went. All signals were in the clear position, very little coal was being used on the fire, and this was unusual with Bert, but on this journey it was sitting on the fireman's seat a lot more than normal.

It was soon past Woking, then Basingstoke, this was probably one of the best and easiest journeys experienced with little coal being used as against other times and steam pressure at near maximum throughout.

Train went through Andover and up the bank to Grately almost as if there was no bank there.

As we motored down through Idmiston Halt, then Porton station, I glanced at the station clock on the up side at Porton – showing 12.00 noon straight up. I checked my watch, something I never normally bothered with – 12 noon. I thought I'd have a word: 'Bert, what's the time?' Out came the pocket watch. Bert looks at it, puts it back in his waistcoat, then almost immediately pulls it out again. Looks a bit puzzled, says to me: 'What do you make it, just turned 12.00?' 'Yes'.

I think Bert was lost for a few seconds, not knowing what to do. He then closed the regulator to shut off steam power to the cylinders. This was previously unheard of, as it was usually approaching Broken Cross that this occurrence took place, Next the vacuum brake was being applied to slow the train down. Train was run now at a slow speed for an express. At Tunnel Junction signals were clear, train was rolled slowly through tunnel to Salisbury and eventually stopped to take water at the end of platform 4 at 12.16pm – seven minutes early.

As usual the train buffs came up and told Bert: 'You know your speed was in excess of 140mph from Amesbury Junction down'. Bert gave his usual reply about printing that. Probably one of the finest journeys undertaken from Waterloo to Salisbury – and Steam!

Over the years I have heard many a tale about Bert Cambray – he was defiantly a speed merchant! Fred was an excellent traction trainer; what he didn't know wasn't worth knowing!

Schools class 828 runs in to Salisbury platform 4 as 70000 *Britannia* stands in the reception road in 1998. (*Paul Abbott*)

Closing Remarks

Mike Pearce, driver at Salisbury

Sadly, we have now run out of room, which is a shame, as we have not run out of stories or photos! Steve and I would like to thank all who have allowed their stories to be told. In October 2008 we had an idea to make a small PowerPoint presentation comprising of photos and stories that we would show on a special social evening to raise some money for charity. Thanks to the vision of publisher Tim Graham, that idea, in only six months, has turned into the book you have just read. He has allowed us to gather the content and present it in a simple, straightforward manner. This book is not an historical or factual record of the past 150 years; it is just an illustration of how proud we, as staff, are in the job we do and the people we work with. No doubt there will be errors in dates and caption details to photos; most photos came with no information, just the photographer's memory. If you would like to comment or add any information please contact me, Mike Pearce, through our publisher (if you want a reply then please enclose an SAE).

Finally I would like to say thank-you to my family, who have been patiently waiting to use our computer for the last four months; my fellow football coaches at Wilton Football Club for taking on the extra training session while I have been sat in the warm writing this book; Steve Chislett, our editor, for his constant encouragement; Tim Graham for the hard work of producing our whim as a Millstream book; all who were mentioned earlier in the introduction; all my workmates for putting up with my constant badgering for photos and stories; and of course you for purchasing this book. Everyone who worked on or contributed to this book did so in the knowledge that all monies raised would go to our chosen charities, including the Salisbury Stars Appeal. Look out for our forthcoming website '72B' at the end of 2009 – and maybe Volume 2!

The nameplate from 34002 *Salisbury*
now hangs on the wall of the Railway Social Club
and is owned by Salisbury Museum.
(*Mike Pearce*)

Index

160